SURPRISINGLY SIMPLE

Novelty Cards

SURPRISINGLY SIMPLE

Novelty Cards

Sue Nicholson

D&C
David and Charles

To Ian, Joshua, Sarah and to the memory of my mum.

A DAVID & CHARLES BOOK
David & Charles is a subsidiary of F+W (UK) Ltd.,
an F+W Publications Inc. company

First published in the UK in 2005

Distributed in North America
by F+W Publications, Inc.
4700 East Galbraith Road
Cincinnati, OH 45236
1-800-289-0963

A catalogue record for this book is available from the British Library.

ISBN 0 7153 1909 4 paperback

Printed in China by SNP Leefung
for David & Charles
Brunel House   Newton Abbot   Devon

Executive Editor   Cheryl Brown
Editor   Jennifer Proverbs
Art Editor   Prudence Rogers
Production Controller   Ros Napper
Project Editor   Betsy Hosegood
Photographer   Karl Adamson

Visit our website at www.davidandcharles.co.uk

David & Charles books are available from all good bookshops; alternatively you can
contact our Orderline on (0)1626 334555 or write to us at FREEPOST EX2 110, David
& Charles Direct, Newton Abbot, TQ12 4ZZ (no stamp required UK mainland).

Contents

Introduction

A novelty card is one that is both fun to make and to receive. It stands out from the crowd, raising a smile or creating a gasp of amazement and it is unique to the giver as well as the recipient. Anyone can make a novelty card, irrespective of ability, and this book, with its simple step-by-step instructions, will show you how.

My first novelty card was the hidden messages card (see page 26). I had been making cards for a number of years, but this one made me realize just how exciting they could be and I was hooked on the concept. Since then I've had great fun creating novelty cards, and I know from family and friends that they were well received.

There are 14 very different cards to make, including favourite ideas such as the pop-up card (page 62), and the slide and pull card (page 72). New ideas that are deceptively easy include a carousel card – card blanks glued back to back (page 38) – or you can make a jigsaw card for a puzzle lover (page 68). With some simple folds you can create a card that 'explodes' when opened (see page 96) or with a bit more time you could make a lovely keepsake box card (page 50).

Illustrated step-by-step instructions enable you to complete each main card exactly as shown, but I'd like to think that you will use this book as a springboard to develop your own ideas. To get you thinking, each card is accompanied by at least one detailed alternative with a photograph and instructions along with other ideas for you to try. There's also a Kids' Korner with several of the designs because your children are bound to want to get involved, and plenty of tips to help with any problems you may encounter.

The cards are not complicated, but I recommend that you practice with scrap paper first to ensure that you understand the construction method. You can also contact me for further advice (see page 111), and I'd love to see a photo of your cards, which I could include on my website.

Happy crafting.
Love, peace, joy and happiness,

Sue Nicholson

noveltycards@suenicholson.com

techniques

This chapter covers the basic techniques of card making and tells you how to select, handle, cut and fold card for professional results. There are also plenty of ideas on embellishment, including making your own stickers or enhancing ready-made ones, using punches and stamps and utilizing papers. Even if you have made cards before, you are likely to find new ideas and helpful tips in this section.

Card maker's tool kit

Before you can begin making cards you will need to collect the tools for the job. This tool kit contains a good selection to cover your needs for all types of card, and is required for the projects in this book.

Adhesives: use a glue stick to secure card to card or card to paper; use PVA with a glue brush when a strong bond is required or when attaching non-paper items.

Cutting mat: self-healing cutting mats are ideal when using a craft knife because they are smooth and flat. They prolong the life of the knife and are easier to cut on than other surfaces.

Bone folder: essential to give sharp, clean creases in card and paper (or use a clean, blunt knife).

Cocktail sticks: for picking up and spreading small amounts of glue or for picking up seed beads.

Craft knife: always use a craft knife with a sharp blade to produce a crisp cut.

Bradawl: for making guide holes in card before using brads. It is available from hardware stores.

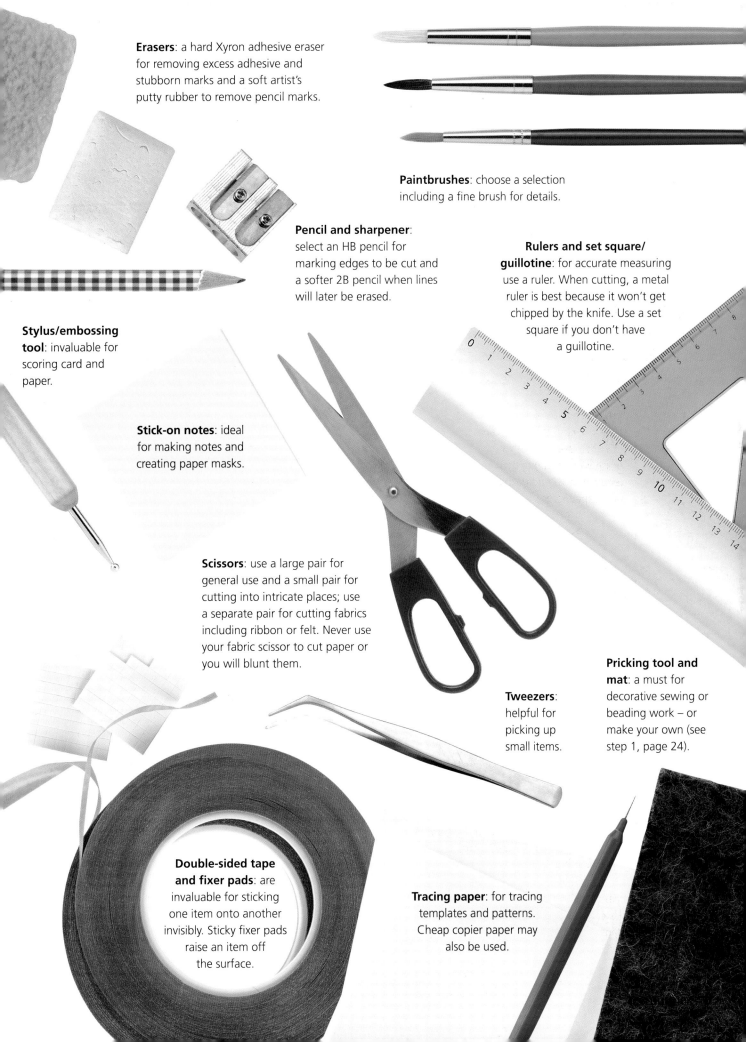

Erasers: a hard Xyron adhesive eraser for removing excess adhesive and stubborn marks and a soft artist's putty rubber to remove pencil marks.

Paintbrushes: choose a selection including a fine brush for details.

Pencil and sharpener: select an HB pencil for marking edges to be cut and a softer 2B pencil when lines will later be erased.

Rulers and set square/guillotine: for accurate measuring use a ruler. When cutting, a metal ruler is best because it won't get chipped by the knife. Use a set square if you don't have a guillotine.

Stylus/embossing tool: invaluable for scoring card and paper.

Stick-on notes: ideal for making notes and creating paper masks.

Scissors: use a large pair for general use and a small pair for cutting into intricate places; use a separate pair for cutting fabrics including ribbon or felt. Never use your fabric scissor to cut paper or you will blunt them.

Tweezers: helpful for picking up small items.

Pricking tool and mat: a must for decorative sewing or beading work – or make your own (see step 1, page 24).

Double-sided tape and fixer pads: are invaluable for sticking one item onto another invisibly. Sticky fixer pads raise an item off the surface.

Tracing paper: for tracing templates and patterns. Cheap copier paper may also be used.

Handling card

Take a little time to understand card and how to fold it properly because a buckled fold can spoil even the most beautiful card. With a little practice you will soon be making your own card blanks, opening up further possibilities, saving money and enhancing your sense of achievement.

Selecting card

The ideal weight of your card is 240/280gsm. If the weight of the card is not given, hold the card in one hand and gently move it (just a little shake). The resistance that you feel should help you to decide whether it will be suitable, too flimsy to stand up or too heavy to fold.

Card grain

Like fabric, paper and card have a grain. The neatest folds are made when they run in the direction of the grain rather than across it. When a fold is made across the grain the top layer can split and look ragged. This can be a particular problem with doubled-sided coloured card or card that has a special finish, such as a pearlized card. Ideally you should cut your card so that the fold will run along the grain. It would be helpful if the grain on A4 (US letter) card and paper always ran from top to bottom. Unfortunately this cannot be guaranteed and you will need to check the direction of the grain for yourself. To find the grain use one of the methods here.

Finding the grain

Partly fold the card first widthways and then lengthways without forming a crease, as shown. Whichever bends more easily is the direction of the grain.

Alternatively, cut a small piece of the card and score and fold it from top to bottom and then from side to side, as shown. The fold made with the grain will be much neater than the one made across it.

mountains and valleys

You may hear card manufacturers refer to mountain or valley folds. Quite simply in a mountain fold the bend of the fold points upwards and in a valley fold it points downwards, resembling a valley.

Cutting card

A paper trimmer/guillotine provides the quickest and neatest means of cutting card accurately. This is a worthwhile investment if you are making all your own greetings cards. Alternatively, measure the card stock to the required dimensions and mark with pencil, using a set square to keep the corners true. Trim the card to size on the cutting mat using a craft knife and metal ruler. Ideally use one continuous cutting movement for each side that you cut.

Scoring card

Scoring card prior to folding breaks the surface fibres of the card, allowing it to be folded neatly and precisely. If you have a guillotine use a scoring blade or run a stylus (embossing tool) along the cutting guide. Alternatively, find the position of the fold with a ruler, use a set square to position it accurately and draw a stylus along the edge.

Making card blanks

If you make your own card blanks you have the option of creating much more imaginative bases for your decorations or you can simply make a standard card in the colour of your choice.

To make a standard blank with a single fold on the left, start by cutting your card stock to the required height by twice the required width. Measure the fold position, halfway across the width, and score the fold line. Gently fold, starting in the middle and working out to the edges. Crease well with a bone folder.

You can use the same basic principles to make card blanks that are tall, fat, square or rectangular, or that have two or more folds, such as the front opening card below.

A front-opening card has its edges meeting in the middle instead of at the side and is an unusual alternative to the standard card. It is used in Lift the Flaps, page 78. You can cut this card as for a standard blank and make the folds half the finished width away from each side edge. However, you have to be very precise to get a good result this way. A surer method is to follow the instructions below.

It is used in Lift the Flaps, page 78.

Making a front-opening card

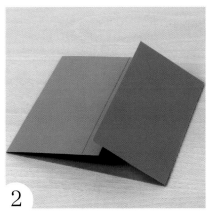

1 Cut the card to the required height by twice the finished width plus 2.5cm (1in). Measure in from the right-hand edge by half the finished width and score and make a fold. Press the fold with a bone folder for a sharp crease.

2 From this fold measure the finished width of the card and score and make a second fold. Fold the left edge in, then the right. Mark where the right side overlaps the left and trim off the excess from the left-hand side.

variations on a theme

On front-opening cards the side panels don't have to meet in the middle. Try making them narrower so the inside shows, or wider so they overlap. They can even be different widths.

Dimensions

When measurements are given for a card in this book the width is given first and then the height, so a card of 10 x 20cm (4 x 8in) is 10cm (4in) wide and 20cm (8in) high.

keeping clean

Protect pale card from marks by placing a piece of copier paper over the top of the card prior to creasing.

Cutting apertures

Sometimes you will need to cut an aperture in your card blank. Cutting the aperture can be done in several ways, and three of the best are given here. Sometimes one method may be more appropriate for the type of aperture you wish to cut but otherwise you can simply choose the method you like best.

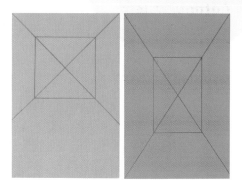

The method given below can also be used to position a square aperture at the top of a tall card or a rectangle within a rectangle.

Straight cut

This method works well for cutting square apertures in paper and card and can be adapted for rectangles of any size. It is also useful when you need to secure a square shape centrally onto another square or a rectangle onto a larger rectangle.

1

Use a ruler to draw light pencil lines from opposite corners of your card square to form a cross. (The pencil lines have been drawn boldly here to make them easy to see.) Where possible draw these lines discretely on the back of the card.

2

Position a ruler or set square between the top arms of the cross and move it up or down. When the measurement between the arms is the same as the required aperture width draw a horizontal line.

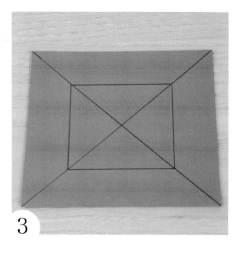

3

Repeat between the bottom arms of the cross and then join the ends of the lines with vertical lines to complete the box. Working on a craft mat, remove the area inside your box – the aperture – using a craft knife and metal ruler.

stencil smart

To cut out several apertures of the same size measure one card square and use it as a 'stencil'. Place it on top of your next card square, ensuring that the sides are lined up, and draw around the inside of the aperture. Then simply cut out.

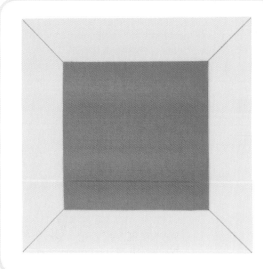

Positioning a square within a square

To position a smaller square centrally on a larger one, first draw the cross on the large square. (Here the pencil lines are drawn boldly so you can see them.) Now place the smaller square on top, lining up the corners with the lines of the cross. Erase the pencil lines afterwards.

Cutting system

With a Coluzzle Cutting System you can cut apertures of any shape or size anywhere on the paper. To obtain good results it is essential to use the correct Coluzzle swivel knife because an ordinary craft knife will not glide through the template channels. You will also need a Coluzzle cutting mat.

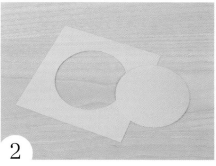

1 Place your card on the Coluzzle mat. Holding the Coluzzle swivel knife in an upright position move it through the channels, cutting the card.

2 The card will be cut to shape, leaving two small uncut areas known as the webs. Use a craft knife or scissors to cut the webs and remove the aperture.

working by numbers

To save time counting the channels on your Coluzzle template, use a permanent pen to write the number of each channel along the webs on the template.

Craft punches

Although most often used to create paper shapes, craft punches can also create fancy apertures, as shown here.

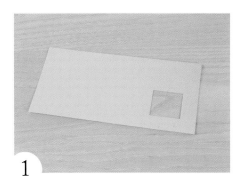

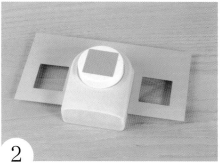

1 Slide the card into the craft punch and press down to cut out the shape. When cutting out three apertures, line up the side of the punch with the top edge to make the first cut. Make the lowest aperture by lining up the punch with the bottom edge.

2 For the final aperture find the centre of the card and mark it. Find the centre of the punch and mark that too, then align the marks to cut out the aperture.

neaten the edges

Tidy up ragged edges of card by rubbing gently with an emery board or nail file.

Experiment with different arrangements of punched windows to create eye-catching and unusual effects. It may help to punch the holes first and then cut the card to size.

Presentation boxes

Novelty cards can be presented in boxes rather than envelopes to prevent embellishments from being flattened or dislodged in the post. You can easily make your own, and it is a nice idea to coordinate it in some way with the card it contains. Follow the steps below to make a rectangular or square box and refer to the boxes opposite for decorative ideas.

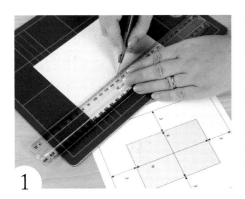

1

Start by making the lid. On scrap paper draw the size of the lid in the centre of your paper and then add the depth of the lid to each side. Measure the full width and length and cut your card to size. Place the card on a cutting mat and measure and mark the depth of the lid along the top long edge. Repeat along the other three edges. Use a ruler and stylus to score along the marked lines.

2

Along one long side, measure from the scored line out by 1cm (⅜in) into one of the corner squares. Draw a guideline from this mark to where the two scored lines cross. Cut up this line and then carefully cut up the adjacent scored line to remove a triangle of card from the corner square. Repeat for the other four corners, as shown. This helps to eliminate bulk and creates neat corners.

a ruler's width

To create a quick box don't bother measuring each side. Instead use the width of your ruler. Take a square or rectangle of card, lay the ruler along one edge and score. Repeat for the other three sides. Proceed to step 2.

wrap it up

Wrap your card in tissue paper or cellophane to make it look extra special and if desired add a layer of bubble wrap above and below the card to keep it safe in the box.

3

Use a bone folder to crease along each scored line.

4

Fold up two adjacent sides and apply glue to the underside of the corner piece. Fold inwards and press into place on the adjacent side. Use a paper clip to clamp the card together while the glue dries. Repeat on the remaining corners. Make the box base in the same way but with the base 2mm (¹⁄₁₆in) shorter and 2mm (¹⁄₁₆in) narrower than the lid to sit snugly inside it. The base sides need to be at least as deep as the lid.

Beautiful boxes

Now you know how to make a basic box you can jazz it up in all kinds of ways to create something really outstanding. After all, the packaging can be part of the gift and can be used by the recipient to keep your card safe or to store any small but precious items.

Fancy ribbon A basic box made from plain card in an attractive colour can be given a further lift with some fancy ribbon. This can be purchased from haberdashers or you can get lovely paper or silk ribbon from florists' shops.

Slotted ribbon This shallow box has been decorated with lovely butterflies that were glued to card, cut out and the wings folded up before gluing in place. Slots were punched in the sides of the lid with a Sizzix paddle punch so that narrow ribbon could be threaded through for an elegant effect.

Short lid The lid of this box is shorter than the base to make a feature of the two sections. The base is simply but effectively decorated with buttons while the lid, which is decorated in a lighter colour, takes its design from the card within.

Three-dimensional decorations Here the use of 3-D stickers has been taken one stage further. The lid has an extra piece of card on top to enable the decorations to stand up on it.

Strengthening papers

Craft stores and scrap-booking suppliers are filled with wonderful decorative papers. Some are sheer or textured like fabric and it would be nice to use them for novelty cards or boxes if only they were strong enough. Luckily you can use them provided that you take some simple steps to strengthen them.

All you need to do is stick the decorative paper onto a second sheet of paper or thin card. White and cream card generally work best under sheer papers because of their light-reflecting qualities. However, do not restrict yourself to these because different colour and pattern combinations can produce some lovely and intriguing results. For best results follow the instructions below.

glittering cover up

If the paper is lacy then areas of adhesive will remain after the paper has been secured. Try shaking glitter or flock onto these areas to cover the excess.

1 If the sheer paper has been creased then flatten it by pressing these areas lightly with a warm iron. Cut the strengthening piece of paper or card and apply adhesive by running it through a Xyron machine or using spray adhesive. (Do not apply glue to the sheer paper because it may wrinkle or crease.)

2 If you have used a Xyron machine remove the backing paper from the card. Lay the sticky paper on a flat surface with the adhesive side facing up and gradually apply the sheer paper onto it. Smooth into place with your hands. The strengthened paper can now be cut and used in the same manner as card.

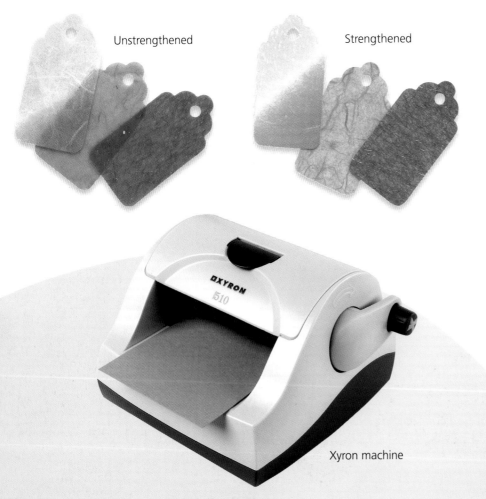

Unstrengthened

Strengthened

Once sheer paper has been strengthened it can be used in the same way as card and you can produce some lovely, unusual gift tags, for example. With a Xyron machine and shape cutter the process is easy.

Xyron machine

Winding templates

Winding card with thread is a popular method of adding decoration. It is easy to do and a variety of effects can be achieved depending on the thread chosen and the method of winding. Look out for random-dyed threads, which can create attractive results.

I create my own templates by using a scallop craft punch but you can also buy Spirelli craft punches, templates and kits designed specifically for winding. Follow the steps below, which show the heart used for the wedding card on page 37, to try out this intriguing technique.

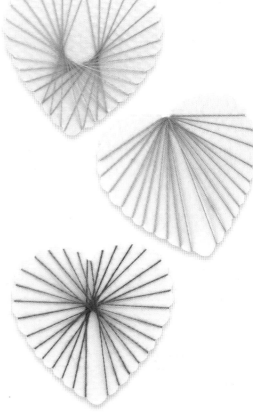

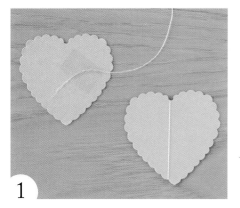

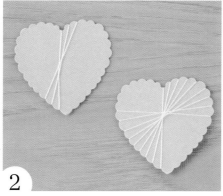

Cut a long piece of thread and use sticky tape to secure the end to the back of your shape. Bring the thread up to the front and through the first valley and take it across to the opposite valley (in this case sixteen valleys to the right).

Bring the thread across the back and bring it out one valley to the right of your start point. Take it across to the opposite side, one valley to the left of the previous thread, and continue in the same way until all the valleys have been threaded. If you need to start a new thread simply tape it to the back of the card. Tape the end of the thread to the back in the same way.

A variety of lovely effects can be produced by winding your card shape in different ways.

decorative detail

If desired, add further decoration to your shape by gluing a button or other trimming to the front. Alternatively, add a sequin as for the wedding card on page 37).

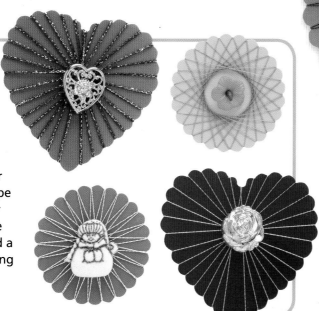

Making and customizing stickers

Stickers are widely available and highly popular with card makers, providing as they do a quick and easy way of adding embellishment. Now you can also make your own with your own choice of paper or card, images in books, magazines, comics, computer clipart, wrapping paper, drawings or even packaging. In fact just about any paper or thin card item can be used.

Once you have chosen your image cut it out roughly, leaving a border all round. Apply adhesive to the back by running the image through a Xyron machine. Now cut out the image exactly. This way you trim off any excess adhesive that may have accumulated around the edges. Leave the backing paper in place until you are ready to use your sticker and then use a pin or pricking tool to separate the sticker from its backing. Your new sticker can either be used as it is or enhanced in one of the ways described opposite.

save it

Part-relief stickers

Some stickers, particularly flowers and butterflies, look effective when parts are lifted up off the surface as on the Easter cards on page 84. To do this, remove the sticker from the protective sheet and turn it sticky side up. From the backing paper cut shapes for the areas of the sticker that will be stuck to the card and put them in place. Dab a little talcum powder onto the remaining sticky areas to cover the glue and strengthen the sticker. Remove the remaining backing and press the sticker in place. Alternatively, apply powder to the entire adhesive area and then glue on the sticker with a spot of glue or a sticky fixer pad.

Make your own stickers from motifs cut from leftover wrapping paper and you'll have the added satisfaction of getting your stickers free.

Enhancing stickers

As well as making your own stickers there are hundreds if not thousands of ready-made ones that you could use to decorate your cards. These are widely available in stationers and toy shops as well as craft stores, and are even sometimes given away with magazines and comics. Some are perfect as they are, but there may be times when you wish to add further embellishment and this is an easy and highly satisfying task. Often the most effective methods are the simplest. For example, add dimension to stickers using puff paint, flocking or liquid appliqué. Alternatively, consider one of the options below.

A touch of glitter Adding glitter immediately gives stickers a lift. Fine, holographic glitter is excellent because it allows the original colours and designs to show through, however the scope here is endless. Try holographic glitter on the wings of angels or use it to add sparkle to water. Try black glitter on a witch's hat and green glitter on Christmas trees.

Button magic Small buttons can often be utilized on stickers, either to emphasize things like car wheels or eyes or to represent themselves. Take a plain letter sticker and jazz it up by gluing coloured buttons onto it, as shown, or accentuate a border pattern.

Ribbon bows Look out for small fabric bows that will add a flourish to a bouquet sticker or jazz up a baby's bib, for example.

Beads and sequins These are excellent for adding sparkle. Pick up the patterns on butterfly wings or brighten up a plain motif by placing one or more sequins artistically on top.

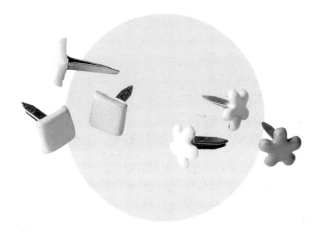

Brads Based on traditional paper fasteners, brads come in many colours and sizes and have become one of the most popular accents for card makers. You can alter a metal brad by drawing on a pattern with permanent marker pens.

Using craft punches

There are many different types of craft punches available, including standard punches designed for cutting borders or small shapes, cassette punches and paddle punches. These can be used to produce shapes, create stencils, add decorative detail or cut apertures.

Standard punches are relatively inexpensive, come in a wide range of designs and are widely available. Sizes range from the very small to super large, with anything from very simple shapes to intricate mosaics. If you experience difficulty punching, try sharpening the punch by using it to cut shapes from cooking foil. If the punch requires more pressure than you can apply, try putting it on the floor and using your foot to apply the pressure.

Cassette punches come with interchangeable cutters in numbers, letters and mini shapes. Very little pressure is required to squeeze the handle, which can be a great advantage. Alphabet and number cassettes can be bought as a set in a carry case or purchased individually so that you can build up a collection over time. Many extra shapes are available such as flowers, hearts and angels.

Paddle punches, available from Sizzix, take punching to a new level because they can punch anywhere on the card, and they can cut through paper, card, foam, thin metal, shrink plastic or fabric. Using these punches is quite straightforward and does not require particular strength or effort.

Using a cassette punch

1

Pull the lever at the base away from the handle and gently push the cassette into the space above.

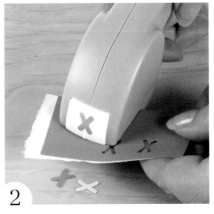

2

Feed the card in to the gap in the cassette and squeeze the handle to punch out. To remove the cassette turn the handle over and lift the lever at the bottom. (This card has been run through a Xyron machine first.)

cassette gauge

Use the handle as a gauge for equal spacing when lining up letters and shapes to produce stencils.

easy stick

Apply adhesive by running card through a Xyron prior to punching.

Using a paddle punch

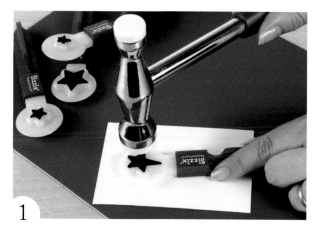

Turn your cutting mat wrong side up so that the imprints left by the punch won't damage the cutting surface. Lay your card on the mat with the punch flat on top. Hold the handle and strike a couple of times with the Sizzix hammer. (This has plastic-covered heads that can be replaced when worn down.)

regular removal

Remove the shapes from your punch frequently because a build up will eventually impair the cutting performance.

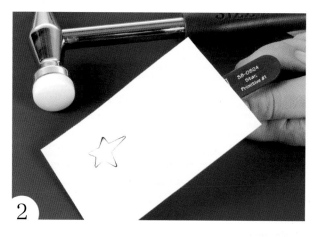

Without removing the punch, turn the card over to check that the blades have come all the way through. If not turn back over, strike and check again.

easy stencil

Paddle punches are ideal for creating small stencils.

When you can see the outline of the blades, remove the paddle punch from the card. Remove the shape by pushing it out with the Sizzix ejector tool or use a stylus.

This card, shown on page 82, features a starry background made with the use of Sizzix paddle punches.

Stamping

This lovely technique is ideal for adding decoration to all your novelty cards, enabling you to transfer a host of different motifs quickly and professionally. It is the perfect choice when you wish to repeat a design several times, both on the card and the envelope or box that contains it, for example.

Your stamp can be inked up with a pad or special marker pens. If you intend to colour the stamped image with a wet medium, such as paints or felt-tip markers, make sure you use a pad with permanent ink to ensure that the outline won't smudge or bleed. Rainbow pads are also available, which can produce pretty effects.

Brush markers

If you wish to produce a stamped image using differed colours – an orange flower with a green stem, for example – special coloured brush markers are the answer. Simply colour each area of the stamp and then press on the paper or card. You'll find it helps if you breathe over the stamp before you press it in place to ensure that the ink is wet because these markers can dry quickly. You can also use these markers to print selected areas of the stamp only, such as a flower without the stem.

rescue remedy

Rescue images that have not turned out correctly by trimming off the smudges to create smaller motifs. Alternatively, cut out the parts that have stamped well and use these in decoupage or to add further interest around your design.

Caring for stamps

- Store ink pads upside down so that the ink sinks to the top of the pad. This ensures that the pad has a nice wet surface for inking up future stamps.
- To avoid the ink drying out or bits of fluff, glitter etc. sticking to your ink pad, always replace the lid immediately after use.
- Clean your stamp regularly with proprietary cleaning fluid or rub it onto a damp stamp-cleaning mat. You can also clean it with alcohol-free baby wipes.

Stamping an image

1
Place the card on a stable, flat surface. Ink up the stamp by tapping the rubber lightly with a dye ink pad until the image is covered. Do not push the ink pad into the stamp as this can result in ink going onto the surrounding rubber. When the image is stamped this ink may then cause unsightly marks.

2
Press the inked rubber onto the card, applying a firm and even pressure. Keep the stamp steady; rocking or moving it may produce unwanted ink marks. Lift up the stamp and leave the image to dry completely.

3
Meanwhile clean your stamp ready for the next use with proprietary stamp cleaner. Dry the rubber by dabbing it onto kitchen paper.

Heat embossing

This technique takes stamping a step further by giving it a raised appearance. It is easy to do. Simply sprinkle embossing powder over a still-wet stamped image, shake off the excess and heat. Now watch the magic happen as the powder slowly melts to produce a raised effect.

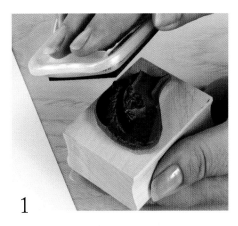

1

Load your chosen stamp with a pigment ink pad in the usual way. Embossing powder can cling to oils transferred from the skin to the card. To help eliminate this, wipe over the card with an antistatic pad before you begin stamping.

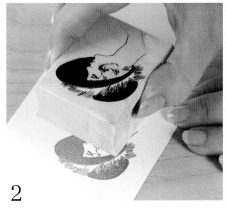

2

Press the stamp onto the card to transfer the image, following the same procedure as in step 2, opposite.

3

Shake embossing powder onto your image and then tip the excess powder off onto a piece of scrap paper with a valley fold. Gently tap your card to remove any misplaced grains of powder and remove any other stray grains with a small, dry brush. Pour the excess powder back into the jar for future use.

4

Melt the embossing powder by heating the card with a heat gun until the powder melts. Slowly wave the heat tool back and forth until the entire design is raised and shiny. Be careful not to overheat. Placing tin foil underneath the card helps the powder melt more quickly but the tinfoil gets hot, so use a clothes peg to hold the card to the foil.

heat from beneath

When using glitter embossing powder it is a good idea to apply heat from underneath. The glitter is only secured when the embossing powder melts but the glitter can scorch before this happens when heated from above.

cutting it out

If you wish to cut out an embossed image always try to leave a narrow border around it. This helps to avoid the risk of it cracking or lifting away from the card.

fine detail powder

If your image loses clarity when embossed, use a fine detail embossing powder instead, making sure you remove any stray grains before applying the heat.

Beads, sequins and charms

Adding three-dimensional objects to your cards helps to make them exclusive and takes them out of the ordinary. As with all aspects of card making, you can take this as far as you like, adding lavish quantities or a selective few, and choosing anything from inexpensive seed beads to extravagant charms. Look out for oddments and mixed selections, which are often inexpensive.

Beads can be stitched to the card with ordinary thread through small holes made with a pricking tool. The neatest way of utilizing sequins is to stitch them on with a small seed bead in the centre, which can be either matching or contrasting. Where possible, charms should be stitched on like buttons through any holes provided. For detailed or complex charms follow the instructions below.

Securing seed beads

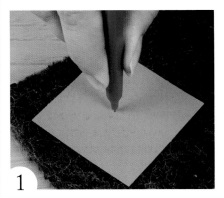

1

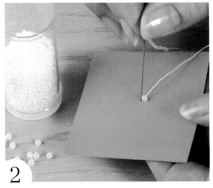

2

Decide where to secure the beads and then place the card onto a pricking mat or piece of dense foam. At each bead position make a hole in the card with the pricking tool or use a needle secured in a cork. (Making a hole first is much easier than attempting to pierce the card with a beading needle.) You may wish to add one bead before deciding where to apply the next.

Thread a beading needle with thread to match the beads and knot the end. Bring the needle up from the back, through the hole in the card. Thread on one bead and take the needle back through the same hole to the back. The bead is now caught in place and covers the hole. Continue adding other beads, keeping the thread taut, then knot off the thread on the back of the card.

Securing sequins

Make a hole at the sequin position as in step 1, left. Thread a beading needle with thread to match the bead rather than the sequin and knot the end. Bring the needle through the hole to the front, thread on a sequin, then a bead and then pass the needle back through the sequin and through the hole in the card. Attach further sequins in the same way. Knot off the thread on the back to finish.

Securing a detailed charm

Select cotton to match the charm, thread it onto the needle and knot the end. (In the photographs contrast thread is used for clarity.) Place the card on the pricking mat or foam and decide where you can attach the charm where the thread is least visible. Make a hole in the card with the pricking tool. Bring the needle up through the hole and through the space in the charm. Pass the thread over the charm and back through the hole. For a large charm you may need to make two holes, passing the thread over the charm from one to the other. Secure the charm as needed.

Using templates

Some of the cards in this book use a template. If you transfer the necessary designs to white card using one of the methods given here, you can produce a sturdy template or stencil for use time and again. Choose whichever method you find easiest or which suits the materials and equipment you have. If you cut the motif out carefully with a craft knife, you can save both portions of the card so that you have a stencil and a template. In some cases you may find it easiest to trace around the inside of your stencil rather than drawing around the template.

Creating a template

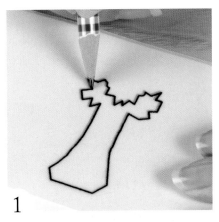

1

Using a sharp pencil, trace the design onto tracing paper or any other paper that you can see through, such as inexpensive copier paper. (This example is the foil from the champagne bottle used for the card shown right and featured on page 44.)

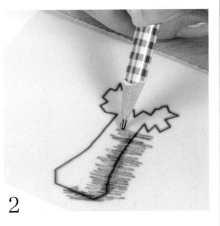

2

Turn over the tracing and place it on some white card. Use a pencil to rub firmly over the outlines of the design, transferring it in mirror image onto the card. Remove the paper and cut out the motif. Turn the template over and label this as the right side.

stencil template

Instead of cutting around a template, use a craft knife to remove the shape from the card. This creates a stencil that can be used in the same way as a template but has the advantage of being see through, enabling exact placement over patterns and designs.

Using graphite paper

Graphite or carbon paper can be used as a quick means of transferring your design to card, wood, metal or fabric. First make a tracing of the template. Place a sheet of graphite paper on your white card and place the tracing paper on top. Now use a sharp pencil to trace over all the design lines, pressing firmly. Remove the top layers to reveal the motif and then cut it out. To avoid confusion label the right side.

Using a scanner or photocopier

If you have a computer scanner you can scan your template into your computer, add text for the label, and then print it out onto thin card. This has the advantage that you can store your template safely for further use and easily enlarge or reduce it to suit your requirements. Alternatively, you can photocopy it directly onto card. Any enlargements can be made by adjusting the percentage of the copy.

This card, from page 44, uses the templates on page 109.

hidden messages

Two strips of card are woven through slits in a card blank to make this intriguing design, which was my first ever novelty card. The card is attractive enough in its own right, but it has a secret that makes it even more appealing because hidden in the card strips is your very own secret message that only the recipient will be able to read.

The nature of this card makes it particularly suitable for a Valentine card, like the one shown opposite, which is decorated in bold red, black and gold as a card for a man. However, your messages don't have to be romantic and on page 31 you'll find some ideas for putting your card to other uses, as a greeting or to cheer up a sick child, for example.

To read the hidden message, open the card and gently push the two woven sections upward to form a 'mountain'. Gently pull apart the woven sections at the top of the mountain to reveal the message. Pull the card out to hide the message again.

As loving as they may be underneath, some men don't like to put their romance on show, and for them this Valentine card is ideal because your sentiments are hidden.

Can you
"reveal" my
hidden
message?

heart to heart

Finished size 14 x 20cm (5½ x 8in)

you will need...

- O Card maker's tool kit, page 8
- O 28 x 20cm (11 x 8in) rectangle of black card
- O Two 6.8 x 20cm (2¹¹⁄₁₆ x 8in) strips of red card
- O Leftover scraps of red and black card
- O A5 shiny gold card
- O A5 white card
- O Folk heart craft punches, large and small
- O Xyron with permanent cartridge
- O Sheet of writing paper and standard envelope so that you can enclose details on how to reveal the hidden message

See also
Making card blanks, page 11
Using craft punches, page 20
Using templates, page 25

card type

Use ordinary card for this project – shiny or double-sided card may separate as you keep folding it. If in doubt, cut a small piece of your card and try folding it several times.

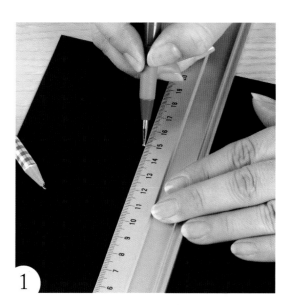

1

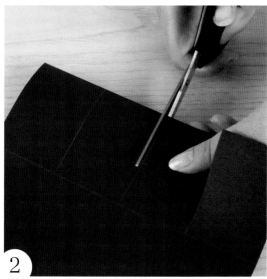

2

Lay out the black card with the short edges at the sides. Create four equal vertical sections by using the ruler to measure across from the left edge to make faint guidelines at 7, 14 and 21cm (2¾, 5½, 8¼in). Score along these guidelines using a ruler and stylus. Fold along each scored line and crease well using the bone folder. Open out the card.

Fold the card blank in half and use the ruler to measure up from the bottom edge. Draw faint pencil guidelines at 5, 10 and 15cm (2, 4 and 6in) from the middle fold to the outer fold. Keep the card blank folded in half and cut from the fold along each of the three pencil guidelines. Do not cut beyond the outer folds.

3

Open up the card blank to reveal three slits between the two outer folds. Check that each slit reaches both folds and lengthen the slits a little more with your scissors if required.

4

To create the woven effect, (and ultimately the hidden message area), take one red card strip and weave it through the slits going under and over. Move this strip all the way over to the left-hand side. Check the width of your strip is correct by ensuring that the middle of the card will still fold. If it won't then the strip is too wide so remove it, trim it and repeat the weaving process. Trim the second strip to match.

5

Repeat the weaving process with the second strip of red card, working on the right-hand side of the card blank and weaving the opposite way for a chequerboard effect.

6

Make a white card template from the tag pattern on page 109. Place it on a piece of leftover red card, trace around it with a pencil and cut it out. Glue the tag onto the black card on the top left-hand side.

mystery message

Write your name and message freehand or use an alphabet stencil. Write on dark card with light coloured gel pens or Galaxy marker pens. You could also punch out the letters of your name and message with an alphabet craft punch set. For the ultimate in mystery, cut your letters and words from magazines.

alternative size

You can make your card any size but keep your calculations simple by cutting your card to a width that is easily divisible by four.

heart to heart

message area

Keep your writing and decoration in the message area no closer to the edge of each rectangle than 3mm (⅛in). This ensures that if the card strips move slightly the edges of you message won't be seen.

7

Punch out eight large red hearts and one black heart from leftover card. Stick these to the card with sticky fixers using the photograph as a guide to placement. Cut the gold card into two and apply adhesive to one half and to more of the red and black leftover card by running them through the Xyron machine. Keep the remainder of the gold card to use later. Punch out twelve black, eighteen red and fifteen gold small hearts, peel off the backing paper and stick in place.

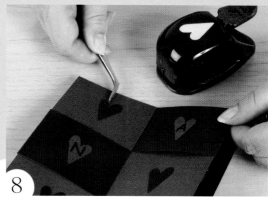

8

Now punch out four black and four red large hearts. Write the letters of your name onto some hearts. Open up the hidden message area of your card as explained on page 26, remove the backing paper and secure these in place. Alternatively, write your message in this area.

second message

There is a second hidden message area. Just turn the card over and with the back facing you open up in the same way. Guide your recipient to this area by writing: "Now can you find the second part of my hidden message?" in the main hidden message area.

9

Punch out four large gold hearts from the gold card you set aside earlier. Fold the Valentine card in half and use sticky fixers to secure these hearts to the front of the card. It is important to decorate this area because this is what will be seen when the envelope is first opened.

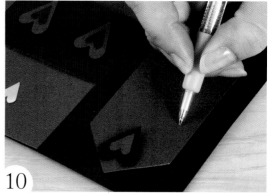

10

On the red tag write: 'Can you reveal my hidden message?' On the writing paper write out how to reveal the hidden message, fold it in half and seal it in the envelope. You can also include a little diagram if you think it will help. On the front of the envelope write 'If you can't reveal my hidden message open this envelope!' Enclose the envelope with your card.

further inspiration

See also
Using templates,
page 25
Using craft punches,
page 20
Strengthening papers,
page 16

Many variations are possible with this card. For example, the four vertical sections do not have to be the same width or shape, so you could make the outer vertical sections wider than the inner ones, creating more space for decoration. For long secret messages reverse this so that the inner sections are wider. If you play around a little I am sure you can come up with a number of ideas to produce hidden message cards that are unique and special.

oriental odyssey Beautiful origami papers and lovely kimono designs give this card a distinctly Japanese flavour. It would make an especially nice greetings card.

Make four equal vertical folds, place a small wineglass onto one outside section and manoeuvre it to create a curve at the top. Draw around the top of the glass with a pencil and then trim away the excess card. Fold the card in half and use this curve as a template for the other outer section. Trim the inner section straight across the top. Prior to cutting the strips for weaving, give stability to the origami paper by backing it with cream card then assemble in the same way as the Valentine card. Use the templates on page 109 to cut two kimonos from the origami paper. Wrap the sash around each body, securing each end on the back with a little glue. Add the sleeves by gluing the inner edge to the body. Glue the kimono to the card, leaving some of the sash and sleeves free for added dimension. Decorate further with flower shapes punched from origami paper and add punched borders.

try this! Draw a trellis on the outer vertical sections and decorate with small dried flowers. Weave in strips cut from floral scented drawer liners to stimulate the senses when the card is opened.

bright idea Bring a smile to a sick child's face by creating a puzzle card. Hide answers and some appropriate jokes in the hidden message area. The child will have great fun showing their card to the other children and nurses.

kids' korner

Make a child's first hidden message card from plain white card woven with coloured card strips. Practice opening and closing the hidden message area with your child and then leave them to decorate it and write messages. Encourage your child to keep their writing and decoration to the middle area of each rectangle. Children can use this card to pass on secret messages when playing imaginary games or budding magicians can astound their audience by using the card for a disappearing trick.

box of delights

Trailing a string of decorations behind it, the lid of this box is lifted up to reveal a streamer of festive fun. As long as they fit in your box, you can attach virtually any card shapes and any number of them to the string, and decorate with additional beads, sequins or whatever you feel fits the occasion. In fact, this is such a versatile idea that you'll probably find a host of reasons to make one and some exciting suggestions are given on page 37.

The principle behind this card is simple though ingenious. A card shape is attached to the top of the lid and the inside of the box base, with a long string of embroidery cotton (floss) or other decorative thread between them. Card shapes are glued to the string with beads strung between them for added decoration. Instructions are given so that you can make the card shown opposite, but as you read through the steps you will see that there is plenty of opportunity for you to add your own twists.

What's in the box? No one could guess the exciting surprise in store when you lift the lid.

What could be nicer than a Christmas card that is personalized for the whole family and doubles as a decoration, perhaps streaming across a mantelpiece or coffee table or draped around the branches of a Christmas tree? This idea would work equally well for a birthday or other celebration.

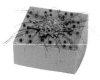

poinsettia parade

Finished size 7 x 7 x 3cm (2¾ x 2¾ x 1³⁄₁₆in)

See also
Presentation boxes, page 14
Stamping, page 22
Heat embossing, page 23
Beads, sequins and charms, page 24

you will need...

- Card maker's tool kit, page 8
- Gold double-sided card cut into three squares, one 13cm (5⅛in), one 12.8cm (5¹⁄₁₆in) and one 6.8cm (2¹¹⁄₁₆in)
- A4 (US letter) sheet of deep red card
- Poinsettia rubber stamp
- Pigment ink pad (gold, tinted or clear)
- Gold embossing powder
- Heat tool
- Fine glitter
- Skein of green metallic embroidery cotton (floss)
- Seed beads in gold and red
- Beading needle
- Tag craft punch, circular craft punch and a small round-hole punch
- Gold alphabet peel-offs or stickers

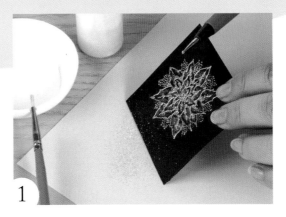

ink it up

Ensure that you re-ink your stamp each time to get a crisp, clear image that the embossing powder will adhere to.

1

Stamp seven poinsettia motifs onto deep red card using the pigment ink pad. Apply gold embossing powder and heat with a heat tool. Use a brush to apply small strokes of glue to some areas of the poinsettia petals. Sprinkle on fine glitter then tap the excess off onto scrap paper and return this to the bottle. Repeat for each poinsettia and put aside to dry.

2

3

Cut out each poinsettia, leaving a small border around the embossing where possible. Cut two 12cm (4¾in) lengths of green metallic embroidery cotton (floss) and split each one into individual threads. Apply a small blob of glue centrally on the back of one poinsettia and arrange the threads crosswise. Repeat five more times and put the poinsettias aside to dry. The seventh poinsettia will be used in the box base and remains undecorated.

Create the box base using the 12.8cm (5¹⁄₁₆in) square of gold card, making the bottom 6.8cm (2¹¹⁄₁₆in) square and the sides 3cm (1³⁄₁₆in) deep. From the larger card prepare the box lid with a top 7cm (2¾in) square and sides 3cm (1³⁄₁₆in) deep. Do not assemble the lid yet but place it on a pricking mat with one poinsettia centred on top. Use the pricking tool to prick holes in the card lid at random around the poinsettia between the threads.

4

Remove the poinsettia and put to one side in the same position. Draw a small arrow pointing to the top on the box lid to help you replace the poinsettia in the original position. Prick a hole in the centre of the box for later use. Thread your needle with a strand of metallic cotton (floss), tie a knot in the end and secure red and gold seed beads to the lid through every hole except the centre one. Aim for a random pattern of colours. Cover up the threads inside the box lid by gluing the 6.8cm (2¹¹⁄₁₆in) gold square over them. Complete the box lid.

5

Punch two red card tags and then punch a small hole at the top of each one. Use gold peel-off letters to add the name(s) of the recipient(s). If the card is going to one person, add a greeting to the second tag or just use one tag.

6

Use the pricking tool to make a hole in the middle of the poinsettia reserved for the base in step two. Thread the needle with a single long strand of green metallic thread and knot the end. Bring the needle up, from the back to the front, through the hole in the poinsettia. Apply glue to the poinsettia and secure it to the inside of the box base. Hold in place until dry.

7

Thread on twenty beads, randomly alternating between red and gold. Push them down to the box base and secure the last bead by taking the thread through it a second time. Leave 6cm (2⅜in) and then thread on a second group of twenty beads, securing the first and last beads by taking the thread through it a second time.

8

Lay out a poinsettia wrong side up and place your thread on top so that the threads on the poinsettia are almost touching the beads. Punch out a red card circle and glue it onto the poinsettia, sandwiching the thread in-between. Leave to dry securely.

even spacing

When using letter stickers, lightly lay the very edge of each letter of the name on a plastic ruler. Start at zero, keeping the spaces even between each one and read off the final measurement. Use this to help you position the letters neatly on the tag.

adding thread

If you find you haven't got enough thread for the string, add another length when you apply the next poinsettia, securing the knot under the card circle.

poinsettia parade

9

10

Starting approximately where the poinsettia's threads touch the main thread, add another group of twenty beads, securing the first and last ones. If you have two tags, attach the first one next. Take the thread through the hole in the tag, around to the back and through it again. Now thread on another bead group.

Secure a second poinsettia to the main thread in the same way as before and then add a bead group. Secure the third poinsettia followed by the second tag using the same method as for the previous tag. Secure two more poinsettias, adding a bead group after each one.

posting it

When sending your box card through the post, cover it with bubble wrap and place it in a strong cardboard box. When delivering it by hand you can pop it in a box or wrap it in tissue paper, if desired.

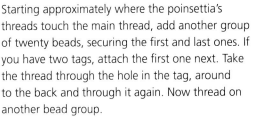

11

12

Now thread on a final bead group approximately 6cm (2⅜in) away from the previous group. Bring the thread up through the hole in the centre of the box top, leaving 9cm (3⅝in) from the last group of beads, and secure on the outside with a knot. Trim any excess thread.

Take the poinsettia you set aside in step 4 and glue it onto the box top, covering the knot and completing the decoration, making sure that it is positioned exactly as before. Place the box base on a flat surface. Hold the box lid up above it and feed the poinsettias and tags into the box one on top of the other, right sides up, in a concertina fashion.

further inspiration

Ring the changes by using a box with an unusual shape, by selecting interesting card for the box or changing its decorations. For quick results work on a ready-made papier-mâché box or buy one already decorated. You can even adapt a box that once contained food or other items. Consider other options for the string too: instead of embroidery cotton (floss) use narrow ribbon, cord, tapestry wool or even chain.

See also
Beads, sequins and charms, page 24
Presentation boxes, page 14
Winding templates, page 17

wedding wishes Made in pearlized card with decorative sequin and bead trimmings, this version makes a lovely keepsake of wedding wishes.

Follow the instructions for the Christmas box but punch out six pink scalloped hearts and enhance each one with a single strand of white metallic embroidery silk to create a Spirelli design. When complete, thread the strand onto a needle, take the needle from the back to the front in the centre and secure a flower sequin. Repeat with the other five hearts. Create a pink box base and cut out the card for a white box top. Decorate the box top with six flower sequins centred on each side. Use a single strand of white stranded cotton (floss) to build up groups of beads, sequins and Spirelli hearts. Glue a square of pink and a smaller square of white card onto the box top. Secure the last heart with sticky fixer pads and add the names or initials of the couple using an alphabet cassette craft punch.

try this! Adapt this card for a milestone wedding anniversary by changing to the relevant colours and decorations. Ask friends and family to write their own anniversary wishes on large punched shapes, and glue a wedding-day photograph to the box lid.

bright ideas
- Create a box card that spells out the recipient's name as the box top is lifted off. You could also include copies of old photographs and tiny envelopes containing little gifts.
- Make a unique family Advent calendar. Make a box card containing twenty-five cards, write the date on each one and add a caption or small picture. Each day pull one more card out of the box and watch as the line gets longer and Christmas day get nearer.

carousel caper

Five cards glued together back to back create a many-sided card that can be viewed from all angles. Once you've read one side turn the card round, then around again like a carousel, revealing a new set of decorations each time. It's ideal if your mind is abuzz with decorative ideas or if you have a set of motifs and can't make up your mind which ones to use. You don't have to restrict yourself – use them all.

The elegant images on the card shown opposite were created by heat-embossing stamped motifs. This is ideal because it allows you to repeat the card again, if desired, but you could easily use stickers as an alternative or even punched motifs and add other enhancements such as buttons or beads. Keep to a theme throughout for a cohesive result or use colour or another linking factor to lead the viewer from one page to the next.

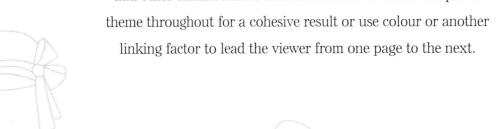

This sophisticated greetings card takes you back to a time when elegance and understated style were captured by the purity of black and white photographs, and it would be ideal for a girl just entering womanhood or anyone with an interest in fashion. A little delicate colouring lifts the concept while maintaining the overall style.

fashionably elegant

Finished size 30 x 20cm (12 x 8in)

See also
Making card blanks,
page 11
Stamping, page 22
Heat embossing,
page 23

you will need...

- Card maker's tool kit, page 8
- Five cream textured folded card blanks 15 x 20cm (6 x 8in)
- A4 (US letter) cream card
- A4 (US letter) burgundy card
- Black permanent dye ink pad
- Black pigment ink pad
- Black embossing powder
- Heat tool
- Variety of couture and text stamps
- Burgundy, blue, yellow and brown marker pens

- Acetate
- Decorating chalks
- Foam chalk applicators
- 1cm (⅜in) wide burgundy ribbon
- Square craft punch

overview

As you decorate the card blanks lay them out in front of you to help you judge the balance of the pages and the overall effect.

1

For this card the insides (with valley folds) of each blank will be on show; the outsides (with mountain folds) will be glued together. Use your stamps and black permanent dye ink pad to stamp images on the inside of each card blank. Leave gaps for the text and embossed images.

2

Use dye ink with the text stamps to fill in any remaining blank areas. Add further interest to the text by stamping at different angles and overlapping. Do this by using stick-on notes to mask off any areas that you do not want to stamp or which have already been stamped.

3

Create a variety of raised stamped images by heat embossing onto cream card. Use the stamps with the black pigment ink and black embossing powder.

4

Scribble the burgundy marker pen onto the acetate and pick up the colour with a damp, (not wet), paintbrush. Add touches of burgundy to both the flat stamped images and the heat embossed ones. Also use this method with yellow and brown marker pens to add colour to the hair and use a blue marker to add colour to the eyes.

The method of scribbling colour onto acetate as described in step 4 also works with ink pads. Dab the colour onto the acetate and then pick up with a damp brush in the same way.

versatile
chalks

Use chalks anywhere you want subtle colour, applying them with your fingertips, brushes, foam make-up applicators, cotton-wool balls or pads, depending on the effect that you wish to achieve and the size of area that you want to colour.

5

Add colour to the women's faces by using a small foam applicator brush to apply a skin-tone chalk. Add a blush to the cheeks and define the lips using a red chalk.

6

Trim around most of the embossed images, leaving a small border to avoid cracking the embossing. Cut the remaining images into rectangles and select a few to be mounted with sticky fixer pads onto burgundy card. Cut the burgundy card into rectangles a little larger than the embossed images and assemble.

fashionably elegant

7

Decide which card blank should act as the front. Apply double-sided tape to the undecorated side of one card and lay 10cm (4in) of ribbon on top. Secure onto the undecorated side of another card, trapping the ribbon in between. Secure the remaining cards together in the same way but omitting the ribbon.

print it

If you don't like your writing style, type the recipient's name on a computer and print it out. Turn the square punch upside down and check whether the name will fit. Alter as necessary and then print out again. Tape a piece of cream card directly over the name, place back into the printer and print again so the text goes on the card, ready for you to punch out.

8

Decide where to add other ribbon details around the cards. Wrap the ribbon around the card so that both ends meet, then glue in place where they will eventually be covered with an embossed image (see the photograph above left). Add the embossed images with glue or sticky fixer pads.

9

Punch a square out of the cream card and use a black pen to write the recipient's name across it from corner to corner. Glue onto the end of the ribbon that was attached in step 7, as shown.

further inspiration

See also
Making card blanks,
page 11
Using craft punches,
page 20

A simple but effective way to adapt this card is to change the number of blanks used to three, four or six. Add a small ribbon loop to the top during assembly so you can hang the card. If you can't glue on all the decorations you'd like to include, you could sew small pockets onto some cards prior to assembly. Another idea is to tie on decorated tags with ribbon that has been threaded through small punched holes near the top.

new baby Instead of stamped images use photographs and punched shapes, such as the Sizzix bottle die featured on this baby card with numbers and letters from a cassette punch. Ribbons and buttons add further detail.

Use four card blanks and trim 2.5cm (1in) from the right-hand side of each one. Die-cut four bottles from pale pink card, add a vellum teat and dark pink rim. Announce the child's name, date of birth, weight and length by punching out letters/numbers from the dark pink paper and securing them to the side of each bottle. Mat each pair of card faces with pink patterned paper, secure a bottle onto one face and a black-and-white photograph on the opposite one. Use a Sizzix paddle punch to create slits down the sides of the wider card faces and weave through pink ribbon. Add pre-cut heart shapes to the ribbon ends and embellish further with buttons and bows. When you assemble the card secure a narrower card face onto a wider one.

try this! Create a fun toy-box shaped card full of toys and games for a child's birthday or one that represents a hamper full of goodies for an adult. Include everything in the hamper from jewels and clothes to cars and holidays. Cut the pictures from magazines or print from the Internet.

bright idea Decorate one card during each day of a holiday to journal activities, meals out, travelling details, weather etc. Assemble and display at home for a reminder of the vacation.

kids' korner

Draw a cross onto the card faces that will eventually be stuck together so that your child does not waste time decorating these. Try creating a colourful card by using five different coloured card blanks. Your child could also try out a different decorating technique for each card face such as using stickers, drawing, collage, painting and potato printing. When complete help your child assemble the card. Consider using glue instead of double-sided tape to make adjustment easier. Do not use too much glue otherwise the card may buckle.

inside out

Passing through an aperture as the card is opened, the feature image of this card transfers from the front of the card to the inside in a beautiful sliding movement. You can have lots of fun choosing the image that will pass through and you can even change the shape of the aperture to suit particular images or occasions (see page 49).

The card has two layers, the outer card blank and an inner lining of folded card or paper, which is secured at both ends but folds inwards at the centre. This construction ensures that any image secured in the correct position will swivel between the front and centre of the card as it is opened and closed. The front of the card can be decorated in the same way as the centre or you could make it completely different as an added surprise.

The champagne bottle is the feature image here and moves to the centre when the card is opened.

Get the champagne corks popping when you send this new year card, full of good wishes. Stamped with party streamers and clocks set at midnight, it captures the excitement of the event and will bring back many fond memories.

new year fizz

Finished size 12.5 x 21cm (5 x 8⅜in)

See also
Making card blanks,
page 11
Using templates, page 25
Stamping, page 22

you will need...

- ○ Card maker's tool kit, page 8
- ○ 24 x 20cm (9½ x 8in) rectangle of white card
- ○ 12.5 x 21cm (5 x 8⅜in) folded red card blank
- ○ 4 x 3cm (1½ x 1¼in) matching rectangle of red card for the label
- ○ A5 white paper
- ○ Leftover of green sparkle card for the bottle
- ○ Leftover of black card for the collar
- ○ Leftover of gold card for the cork
- ○ Leftover of gold vellum for the foil
- ○ Clock face and hands rubber stamps
- ○ Confetti background rubber stamp
- ○ Black permanent ink pad
- ○ Gold peel-off numbers
- ○ Sticky dots
- ○ Glitter glue
- ○ Marker pens in brown, beige and vibrant colours

stick-on masks

When making a mask for a stamp, such as the clock face, simply stamp the image on a stick-on note, making sure you include some of the sticky area of the paper. Cut out the image and position on your work to protect it.

1 On the white card start to create the background by stamping four clocks with hands set to midnight. Use the clock face and hand stamps with the black permanent ink pad. Stamp a fifth watch onto the A5 white paper and put to one side. Create two stick-on note masks of the clock face (see the tip, left) and stick over two of the clocks on the background. Fill the background with confetti using the confetti stamp with the black permanent ink pad. Move the masks to the other clocks as you progress.

2 Use the beige and brown marker pens to colour in all five clocks. Use more vibrant marker pens to add colour to the confetti background.

3 Divide the decorated background card into four equal vertical sections. From one side measure in at 6, 12 and 18cm (2⅜, 4¾ and 7⅛in) and draw faint guidelines. Score with a stylus and ruler.

4

Fold the background card in half and measure 1cm (⅜in) up from the lower edge. Draw a guideline from the centre fold to the first fold. With the card still folded in half, cut along the guideline. Do not cut beyond the first fold. Create a 1cm (⅜in) strip at the top in the same way.

5

Cut an aperture in the far left vertical section aligning it with the fold. The aperture is 14cm (5½in) high and 4.5cm (1¾in) wide. It is positioned along the fold and 3cm (1³⁄₁₆in) in from the top and bottom edges.

6

Lay the background card centrally onto the red card blank, lining up the centre folds. Make a pencil mark at both corners on the right-hand side. Apply double-sided tape under both the 1cm (⅜in) strips and to all four sides of the far right vertical section. Keep the tape close to the outer edges and the fold. Line up with the centre fold and corner marks then press into place.

7

Lay the card out flat and use a pencil to trace through the aperture onto the red card underneath.

quick work

If you are in a hurry, use a printed background card and stamp the clocks onto a tinted paper, cut out and stick them on.

wait for it

Do not trace through the aperture in the background card until it is secure. Doing this earlier can result in misalignment.

new year fizz

There are a number
of options available
to secure vellum
without the glue
being visible. Use
sticky dots or pads or
apply adhesive using
a Xyron machine.

8

hold it!

Before permanently
securing the bottle,
use blue tack to
secure the bottle
temporarily. Check
that the angle looks
correct from both
the front and the
inside and adjust
as necessary.

Flip back the background card and cut the aperture from the red card. Lay the
background card over the card blank so that both apertures line up. Apply
double-sided tape along the top, bottom and side edges of the left vertical
section. Apply to the area above and below the aperture up to the fold. As before
keep close to the edges and the fold.

9

10

Make a template of the champagne bottle on page
109. Trace and cut out a green bottle, black collar,
gold cork and gold vellum foil. Using the sticky dots,
secure the foil and collar in place. Use double-sided
tape to stick the red rectangle to the bottle. Add
the date using peel-offs and decorate the collar by
adding a zero. Place the bottle to the left of the
centre fold so that the bottle neck is within the
aperture. Check that you are happy with the angle
then secure it to the background card with sticky
fixer pads. Put the cork to one side.

Close the card so that the champagne bottle
revolves to the front. Cut out and glue on the fifth
clock. Use sticky fixer pads to secure the cork,
adding black lines for movement and glitter glue
for sparkle.

further inspiration

See also
Making card blanks,
page 11
Using templates,
page 25

This card can be adapted in many ways. Not only can you change the card's background but you can also use a different object in the aperture. If you are feeling adventurous, cut the aperture in a more exciting shape, as for the sailing card below, using a shape cutting system such as Coluzzle for best results. Make sure that whatever you do you keep the aperture within the far left vertical section and align it with the fold.

plain sailing Watercolour paints and peel-off stickers are used to add style and colour to the card in record time. The yacht sails through a half-moon aperture cut with a Coluzzle cutter.

Stick the lighthouse, buoy and yacht onto white card painted with watercolours. Score and fold this background paper and use the Coluzzle cutting system to cut a semicircular aperture near the bottom. Using a small hole punch, create a random effect of holes in the two inner vertical sections. Secure the blue paper to blue card and cut the aperture so that the curve is slightly smaller than on the background. Secure the background in the same way as on the new year card. Cut out the peel-off stickers and secure with sticky fixer pads. Add lots of seagull peel-offs and enhance these with a little glitter glue. Decorate the front with a tag, (see the tag template, page 109) and add the recipients' name. Add more sailing items and seagulls from the peel-off sheet. Use gold peel-off strips to draw attention to the aperture.

try this! For a feminine card create a garden full of pretty flowers with butterflies and bees dancing above. Stick a peel-off greeting onto a large punched flower shape and use as the moving image.

bright ideas
- Glue a photo of a golfing friend swinging their club onto a piece of card and use this as the moving image. Decorate the background to represent the green and hitting a hole in one.
- Create a belated birthday card by using a moving die-cut elephant. On the front write 'This elephant didn't forget your birthday' and inside write 'but I did. Sorry!'

open sesame

A present in its own right, this card doubles as a lovely keepsake. Inside are three mini cards, an envelope and a smaller box that can be used to record important information and store small but precious items, such as a lock of hair or a baby's first tooth. It's ideal for recording a birth or wedding, but it has a host of other uses too, such as a mini play scene or a three-dimensional Halloween card (see page 55).

The intriguing box is 'locked' by a clever ribbon and bead system. Only when the recipient slides down the bead and loosens the ribbon do the side panels fall outwards to reveal a delightful record of a birth, marriage or any other occasion. When time is on your side, try making your own objects to go inside from clay, paper, fabric and beads. When it isn't then look for readymade items among the almost limitless number of doll's house accessories and cake decorating pieces that are available.

Lift the lid and release the bead to reveal a celebration of a birth and a lovely keepsake.

Celebrate the birth of a baby boy, adding his name and the time and date of his arrival to the inside flaps. Special wishes for the child can be tucked into the gingham pocket and the small box could be used in future to store his first lost tooth or a lock of hair. This unusual card will be cherished for many years to come.

new baby boy

Finished size 8.5 x 8.5 x 8cm (3⅜ x 3⅜ x 3¼in)

See also
Making card blanks,
page 11
Cutting apertures, page 12
Strengthening papers, page 16
Presentation boxes, page 14
Beads, sequins and charms,
page 24
Using craft punches,
page 20

you will need...

- ○ Card maker's tool kit, page 8
- ○ White card cut into five 8cm (3¼in) squares; three 3.5 x 7cm (1⅜in x 2¾in) mini folded cards; one 9.5cm (3¾in) square; one 9.3cm (3⅝in) square and one 14.5cm (5¾in) square plus an additional A4 (US letter) sheet of card
- ○ Gingham wrapping paper cut into four 7.5cm (3in) squares; four 5cm (2in) squares; four 1 x 8.5cm (⅜ x 3⅜in) strips; one 6.5 x 5cm (2⁹⁄₁₆ x 2in) rectangle; one 9.5cm (3¾in) square and some leftover scraps
- ○ Craft punches – foot, hand, small heart
- ○ 5mm (¼in) hole punch and hammer
- ○ 2m (2yds) of 3mm (⅛in) wide white ribbon
- ○ Sewing needle and white cotton
- ○ Three small white teddy bear buttons with shanks
- ○ Four small white beads
- ○ Small white bow
- ○ Small and large white pompons
- ○ Computer and colour printer or attractive blue pen

preparation is all

You'll find this card goes together much more smoothly if you cut out all the pieces before you begin so that you don't have to keep stopping to cut the next piece once construction is under way.

1

Make a box side panel by gluing a 7.5cm (3in) gingham square centrally onto an 8cm (3¼in) white card square. Create two more side panels in the same way. (The final panel will be made later on.)

2

Print the name of the baby, the time and date of birth onto white card from your computer or write them on with blue pen. I used the Funstuff font and a clock to depict the time in light blue with a dark blue outline. Ensure that each text element will fit on your mini cards then trim around each one. Use sticky fixer pads to secure each element to one mini card.

3

Cut 20cm (8in) of white ribbon, fold it in half, crease and open up. Apply two or three rows of double-sided tape to the bottom back of one mini card. Lay the ribbon down the centre of the card back with the ribbon crease on the mini card fold. Press the ribbon onto the tape. Add ribbon to the other two mini cards in the same way.

4

Make a pencil guideline 1.5cm (⅝in) from the back of one side panel. Secure a mini card to the panel so that the fold is on the guideline. Cut both ends of the ribbon to a point and feed through a white bead. Push the bead towards the mini card. Measure 8cm (3¼in) down each piece of ribbon; tie a knot in the end and trim. Add mini cards to the other two side panels in the same way. Add a bear button to each side panel by stitching it on in the same way as a bead. Add a dab of glue for strength.

5

Apply double-sided tape to the bottom and sides of the 6.5 x 5cm (2⁹⁄₁₆ x 2in) rectangle of gingham paper and glue onto the remaining side panel to make a pocket. Glue the small white bow to the front, as shown.

use a Xyron machine

You can stick the paper to the card by using a Xyron machine to apply adhesive. For best results run the gingham paper through the machine before cutting out the pieces.

6

Use the 9.3cm (3⅝in) white card square to create a small box with a base of 3.3cm (1¼in) square and sides 3cm (1³⁄₁₆in) deep. Strengthen the 9.5cm (3¾in) gingham square by securing it to the matching white card square. Use it to create the box lid with a 3.5cm (1⅜in) top. Glue the small white pompon on top of the gingham lid.

7

The remaining 8cm (3¼in) square is the base. Draw a faint pencil cross on the square to assist in positioning the small box and then secure it centrally using double-sided tape. Erase the pencil lines.

8

The box is hinged together using the 5cm (2in) gingham squares. Score one square from corner to corner, fold, open up and apply glue to one half. Lay the base square centrally on top so that the edge is in line with the fold and press into place.

new baby boy

9

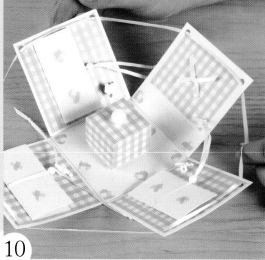

10

Apply glue to the other half of the square, place the pocket side panel on top, aligned with the base, and press to stick. Leave a minute gap between the base edge and the side panel edge to allow the panel to lift up. Place the base so that the pocket panel is at the front. Working clockwise, glue the name side panel, the time side panel and the date side panel to the base in the same way. Ensure that the mini cards are front facing before securing. The photograph above shows what the panels look like from the back.

Punch a small hole into the top corners of each side panel. From leftover gingham paper, punch out sixteen hearts, two hands and two feet. Glue these to the base, side panels and mini cards. Starting with the pocket side panel, thread the remaining white ribbon in and out through the punched holes so that it runs across the decorated inner panel out through the holes and then in and over the next panel. Raise the panels to form a box by gently pulling the ribbon.

added details

To personalize the card further, consider adding the weight of the baby and any other details such as his length, the colour of his eyes and hair and his zodiac sign.

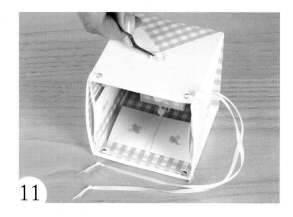

11

12

Cut both ends of the ribbon to a fine point and feed through the remaining white bead. Push the bead up towards the top so that the box closes and tie a knot in each end of the ribbon. Punch out and glue a gingham heart to the top point of each triangle.

Use the 14.5cm (5¾in) white card square to create the opening box card lid with a top of 8.5cm (3⅜in) and sides of 3cm (1³⁄₁₆in). Glue the remaining 7.5cm (3in) gingham square to the lid and use a blob of glue to secure the large white pompon on top. Add further decoration by gluing a gingham strip to each side, trimming any overlap with scissors. Cut a small notch 2.5cm (1in) up one corner to accommodate the bead closure when the lid is in place.

further inspiration

See also
Making card blanks,
page 11

With this card there is scope to include items that would normally be unsuitable. For example, if you enjoy making little clay models or can knit or sew small scale, then this is a wonderful way to incorporate your talents into card making. Another adaptation idea is to change the shape of the box to a rectangle or work with hexagonal or octagonal bases.

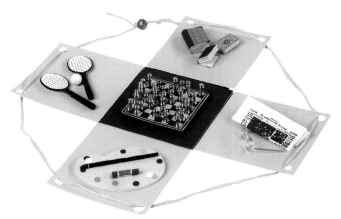

feminine charm
Doll's house accessories are used here to create the scene, along with a necklace and earrings created with small flat-backed pearls.

This card is made from cream pearlized card cut to the same dimensions as the baby boy card. Each square is matted with a coordinating paper and the doll's house accessories are secured on top with double-sided tape or glue. Flat-back pearls were glued in a circle to resemble a string of pearls with two more glued alongside as matching earrings. The ribbon closure is tied in a bow.

try this!
Send special congratulations to a friend who has recently passed their music exams. Secure a small doll's house piano to the centre square and surround it with miniature music scores and musical note stickers on the side panels.

boys' toys
Fill this card with images that relate to your father's favourite hobbies. Doll's house accessories are ideal for this; here they have been secured to the base and side panels with double-sided tape and glue.

Use 6cm (2⅜in) squares cut from yellow/blue double-sided card for this box card. Each panel depicts one hobby as illustrated with a doll's house accessory. The lid is decorated with punched musical notes and the greeting can be written on the top of the box lid. Add a bead closure and knot each end. Note that the bead closure is a little different to that on the new baby boy card because one end of the raffia thread is fed through the hole from top to bottom and the other is threaded from bottom to top.

bright ideas
- Seek out teeny weenie play people, teddy bears, cars or trains. Design a fun house or village theme card for a child that can be played with for weeks to come.
- For a surprise Halloween greeting, create a rectangular opening box card decorated like a coffin. Complete the effect by adding a glow-in-the-dark skeleton, gravestones and lots of plastic spiders.

pocket present

Ideal for gift vouchers or money, this card has a handy pocket on the front that can be made any size or cut at any angle (see pages 60–61). It helps to show that our choice of gift has been carefully thought out and that we are prepared to give time as well as money to the recipient and it demonstrates how much we are thinking of them.

It's great fun thinking of ways to decorate this card in a way that links in with the type of voucher. The card opposite would be ideal for a gardening voucher or for a general voucher for a child who loves nature. Alternatively, you can decorate it to suit the occasion, such as a graduation (see page 60), birthday or wedding.

The card looks just as good without the gift envelope as with it.

This funky bug card has a hidden pocket that is concealed within the lines of the patterned backing paper, so make sure your voucher peeps over the top of the pocket. Ready-made stickers, flower-shaped brads and punched flowers enhanced with seed beads provide the decoration.

say it with flowers

Finished size 14 x 21cm (5½ x 8⅜in)

you will need...

- ○ Card maker's tool kit, page 8
- ○ 14 x 21cm (5½ by 8⅜in) folded orange card blank
- ○ A4 (US letter) orange card
- ○ Two 13 x 20cm (5⅛ x 8in) identical rectangles of striped paper
- ○ Daisy craft punches, large and small
- ○ Orange permanent marker pen, such as a Galaxy marker

- ○ Pale green seed beads
- ○ Bug stickers
- ○ Yellow flower-shaped brads
- ○ Small red envelope for the gift voucher
- ○ Bradawl

See also
Making card blanks, page 11
Using craft punches, page 20

1

2

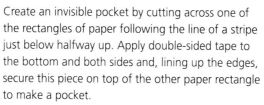

Create an invisible pocket by cutting across one of the rectangles of paper following the line of a stripe just below halfway up. Apply double-sided tape to the bottom and both sides and, lining up the edges, secure this piece on top of the other paper rectangle to make a pocket.

Using the permanent marker pen, add a small circle of orange to the centre of each yellow flower brad. Put aside to dry.

decorating brads

Only permanent pens dry on shiny surfaces and do not smudge or come off when handled. If you don't have a suitable pen to decorate the brads, glue on a small, flat-back gem instead or use a sticker.

3

Lay the striped background paper centrally on top of the card blank. Use a bradawl to make a hole in one corner through both the paper and card. Push a brad through the hole and secure by opening up the wings. Use scissors to trim the wings if they protrude over the edges of the card. Repeat for the other corners.

4

Place the envelope in the pocket at an angle to see where it will sit. Use tweezers to help you handle the stickers and place them on the card in a pleasing arrangement. If desired, add a sticker behind the voucher to ensure that the card still looks good when it has been removed.

5

Punch eleven small daisies from the orange card. Dab a small blob of glue on the centre of one using a cocktail stick. Pick up a seed bead with another cocktail stick and push it onto the glue with a third stick. Repeat for the remaining daisies and put aside to dry. Now punch three large daisies from the orange card and glue an arrangement of beads in the centre.

6

Glue a small daisy to one corner of the gift voucher envelope and the remaining daisies to the card. Your card is now ready to send.

design
check

From time to time take the envelope out of its pocket to see what the design will look like once the recipient removes it.

further inspiration

For simplicity the pocket of the garden voucher card runs straight across the background, but you can cut and position it however you like, as you can see in the examples below. As an alternative you can add your pocket to the inside or the back of your card.

See also
Making card blanks, page 11
Using craft punches, page 20

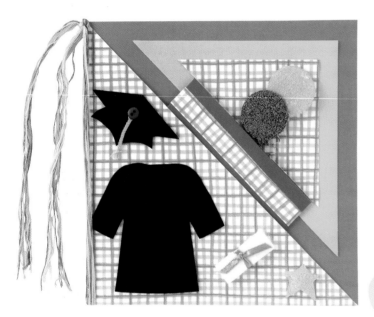

graduating colours
Bright card and checked paper team up with ready-made stickers to create this cheerful greeting.

Make a folded square orange card blank. Take a square of checked paper cut to the same size as the card front and cut in half diagonally. Secure the side and bottom of the triangle using double-sided tape. Cut a smaller triangle from yellow card and an even smaller one from the leftover checked triangle. Secure with double-sided tape. Coordinate the gift envelope by adding a strip of checked paper along the outside edge. Add ready-made stickers and tie a mix of orange and yellow threads around the fold, like the tassels on a mortarboard as the finishing touch.

 try this! Send congratulations to a learner driver who has just passed his or her driving test. Use paper that resembles road markings and add handmade amusing road signs. Write 'Learner Driver' on the gift envelope and then underneath it write 'Congratulations. You've passed!' When the gift envelope is removed your sentiment is revealed.

 bright ideas

• For an avid reader, create a pocket along the bottom of your card that resembles shelf of books. Write some fun titles on the spines, omit the envelope and instead pop a matching bookmark in the pocket.

• Send out a special handmade Christmas tree decoration with your cards this year. Add a simple pocket to your card design to hold the decoration.

• Send special retirement wishes by adding extra pockets to the inside of your card. Pop in gift vouchers, photos of office celebrations or individual notes from colleagues.

• Use vellum or cutaway pockets on you scrapbook pages so that they partly reveal what they hold. Use to store precious mementoes such as tickets, hand-written notes, gift tags plus extra photos.

bright ideas

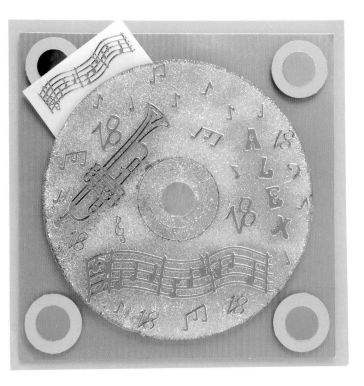

sound idea Most teenagers appreciate a music voucher as a present. Decorate an old or free CD with lots of glitter and peel-off stickers to make the wishes sent with this card sparkle.

Make a folded square lime card blank and use sticky fixer pads to secure a slightly smaller square of silver striped card on top. Apply adhesive to the shiny side of the CD by running it through a Xyron. Decorate with silver peel-off stickers and then shake on lime and yellow fine glitter. Secure to the silver card with sticky fixer pads only placed around the bottom half. Punch out four medium-sized circles from lime card and glue on smaller circles punched from silver card. Secure to each corner using sticky fixer pads. Add a toning gift envelope decorated with a peel-off sticker.

try this!

Just for fun, send vouchers to a college student living away from home in a card decorated with their favourite breakfast cereal. Place a small plate on an empty packet, draw around it and cut out. Alternatively, create a collage of paper food wrappers and then cut a circle in the same way. Add some fun comments and pop in the post with a cheque or vouchers to make the recipient's day.

kids' korner

This is such an easy card for children to make and they are certain to have lots of ideas about fillings. I suggest making a larger card with children by folding an A4 (US letter) card in half. The pocket can be made large enough to hold a few items. Decide on the pocket shape, cut it out and help your child to assemble the card. The type of things that your child might like to put into the pocket may include small packet of sweets, plastic insects, popular trading cards, balloons, play jewellery and stickers plus small party favours such as mazes, puzzles and packs of beads.

✔ thank you

For a friend or relative that lives far away, help your child make a personal thank you pocket card. When complete, pop a photo of your child opening their gift into the pocket.

perfect pop-ups

A true perennial favourite, the pop-up card is loved by children and adults alike. Even when we have learnt how it works, there is still something magical about the way that the image rises up when the card is opened and then folds flat again when it is closed. There is also something very pleasing about a three-dimensional card.

The card shown opposite has all the pop-up decorations fixed to one strip so that they all rise up together. However, once you have mastered this style of card you can easily add further strips. The birthday card on page 67, for example, has two strips on it for a double layer of candles on the cake. These cards utilize die-cuts to speed up their manufacture, and with so many designs at your disposal, as well as the opportunity to cut out your own card shapes, there is no limit to the variations you can design yourself.

Who could guess what is inside this card? The key is a clue.

This new-home card sends bright and sunny wishes to a couple moving house, though by adding some doll-style elements it could easily be adapted to suit a small girl for a birthday. Die-cut and punched shapes help to create the card quickly and effectively.

Thomas
&
Claudia

home sweet home

Finished size A5 (4 x 5¾in)

you will need...

○ Card maker's tool kit, page 8

○ Sizzix die-cutting machine

○ Sizzix dies – green tree and yellow picket fence

○ Small hole punch

○ Mini flower punch

○ Xyron machine with permanent cartridge (or spray adhesive)

○ 50cm (19½in) of yellow embroidery cotton (floss)

○ Two small silver key charms

○ Computer and colour printer (or attractive pen)

○ **Lime green card**: an A5 (4 x 5¾in) sheet; 21 x 15cm (8⅜ x 6in) rectangle for the grass; 3 x 28cm (1½ x 11in) strip for the pop-up; 14 x 11cm (5½ x 4⅜in) rectangle for the tree

○ **Brown card**: 9 x 5cm (3⅝ x 2in) rectangle for the house wall; 1 x 3cm (⅜ x 1½in) rectangle for the chimney; 14 x 11cm (5½ x 4⅜in) rectangle for the tree

○ **Dark red card**: two A5 sheets; 1.5 x 3cm (⅝ x 1½in) rectangle for the door; 1.5cm x 3mm (⅝ x ⅛in) strip for the window

○ **Beige card**: 3 x 10cm (1½ x 4in) rectangle for the roof; 11 x 7cm (4⅜ x 2¾in) rectangle for the picket fence

○ **Lemon card**: A4 (US letter) sheet; A5 sheet; 1.5 x 3cm (⅝ x 1¼in) rectangle for the window; 1.5 x 15cm (⅝ x 6in) strip for the pathway

See also
Making card blanks, page 11
Using craft punches, page 20

rescue it

To rescue a pop-up that accidentally protrudes from the side of your card, simply glue your card onto a larger card blank, adding more width or height to cover it. Use a contrasting card blank so it appears to be part of the design.

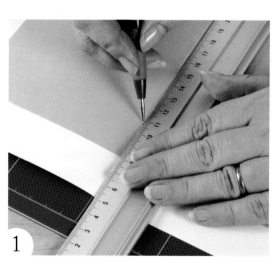

1 Lay the green grass rectangle centrally on the A4 lemon card and mark each corner in pencil. Glue the green card in place using the pencil marks as a guide, covering all of the back with glue, not just the edges. Use a ruler and stylus to score down the centre of the cards for the main fold and erase the pencil marks.

2 Die-cut the beige card fence, one brown card tree and one green tree. Remove the top from the green tree and glue onto the brown one. Apply adhesive to one A5 red card sheet by running it through the Xyron. Use the small hole punch to punch out nineteen small circles. Stick eleven on the tree and put the remaining eight to one side. To create a true roof shape cut off the sides of the beige roof card at an angle. Glue onto the brown wall card, overlapping by approximately 1cm (⅜in). Glue the brown chimney, red door, lemon window and red window strip in place. If necessary, trim the brown wall card that protrudes from behind the slanted roof.

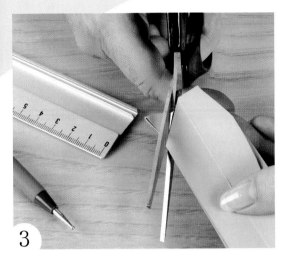

3

Take the green pop-up strip, measure up 1.5cm (¾in) from the shortest side, score with a stylus and crease with a bone folder to create a long fold. Fold in half lengthways and crease with a bone folder. Open up and trim along one long edge so that it is wavy to resemble bushes and hedges. Find the centre point by folding in half and creasing well. Measure 1.5cm (¾in) from this fold along the strip and make a pencil mark. Cut at an angle from this mark to the straight edge of the strip, as shown, to remove a triangle. This helps the pop-up strip move more freely.

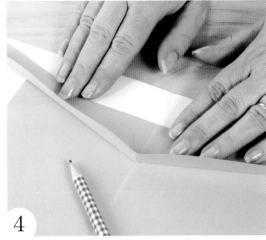

4

Measure 3.5cm (1⅜in) from the back of the green grass card up the fold and make a pencil mark. On the house side of the grass only draw a pencil guideline from your mark to the back corner of the green card. Hold the pop-up strip on the card, notch side down and with the fold aligned with the fold in the card, as shown. Line up along the guideline and mark where it crosses the edge of the green card. Trim off the excess and then fix in place with double-sided tape. Hold the other side of the strip so that it crosses the opposite corner in the same way, mark and remove the excess but do not fix in place yet.

fold and stick

I find it preferable to secure the second half of the pop-up strip by closing the card onto it. If this strip is secured when in the upright position the pop-up does not always fold down properly. Try experimenting with both options to see which works best for you.

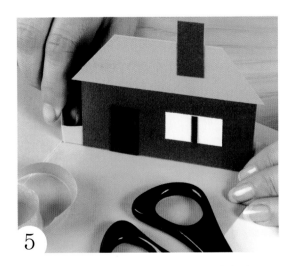

5

Apply double-sided tape to the bottom of the house and secure this to the pop-up strip. Glue the tree trunk and the picket fence onto the other side of the strip. Apply double-sided tape to the unsecured side of the pop-up strip but do not remove the backing paper yet.

6

Lay the house down against the card, as it will be when the card is closed. Lay the tree side on top of it, keeping it at the same angle. Remove the backing paper from the double-sided tape and, holding the pop-up in place, fold the other side of the card down on top. Both sides of the pop-up strip are now secured.

home sweet home

7

no printer?

If you don't have a printer you can easily write the necessary wording freehand. Alternatively, use rub-on letters, stickers, peel-offs or rubber stamps.

Lay the yellow pathway strip from the door at an angle. Mark where it crosses the green grass card, trim off the excess and fix in place with double-sided tape. From the red card that has been run through the Xyron machine, punch seventeen small flowers and stick along the path and under the window.

keep the surprise

Pop-up cards do not close completely flat. By tying it closed you not only make the opening of the card a little more special but also keep it from popping open on its own and spoiling the surprise.

8

9

Type the wording on your computer and print onto paper. Make any necessary adjustments to the font size so that it fits within a rectangle 8 x 9cm (3¼ x 3⅝in). When you are satisfied, tape the A5 sheet of lemon card over the text, place it back into the printer and print again onto the card. Trim the text into a rectangle. Alternatively, write the wording in pen. Cut a slightly larger rectangle from the second sheet of A5 red card. Fix to the card using double-sided tape and then secure the yellow card on top. Glue a silver key centrally to the bottom. Secure your remaining eight red circles to look like fallen apples.

Print out your wording again, but this time onto the green A5 card. Trim into a rectangle and glue the second silver key charm centrally at the bottom. Wrap the yellow embroidery cotton (floss) around the card and trap in place by securing the green card over the top with sticky fixer pads. Tie in a bow and trim the ends.

further inspiration

See also
Making card blanks,
page 11

Pop-ups can be adapted for almost every occasion and every theme. All you have to bear in mind is that the pop-up image stands up correctly and does not protrude from the sides of the card when it is closed, giving the game away. Making a simple mock-up of your design first helps cut out the guess work.

you've passed! Made from grey card with a Sizzix die-cut car, black stickers and paper, this card is huge fun and just right for someone who has just got their driving licence.

Take a 10 x 15cm (4 x 6in) grey card blank and glue on grass-effect paper at an angle from the front corners so it is 7cm (2²/₃in) wide at the back. Apply two black peel-off strips to each side of the grass to create the effect of a kerb and draw black dashes on the fold to denote the middle of the road. Die-cut one red car and then add black trimmings by die-cutting a second car in black, cutting off the pieces and securing to the red card. Add black peel-off smiley faces to the headlights, fold the car in half, and secure to a grey pop-up strip. Spell out the driver's name with large black stickers.

 try this! Adapt this card by using the Sizzix bus decorative die to create a good-luck card for a student or teacher who is starting at a new school. Ask everyone to sign on either the grass verge or road.

18 today This card shows how the pop-up can be altered to have the centre of the pop-up strips pointing to the back instead of to the front. Decorate the pop-up strips to resemble an iced cake and then secure Sizzix die-cut candles on each one.

Make a large card blank by folding an A4 (US letter) pink card in half. Make two pop-up strips, use scissors to create decorative edges on a deeper pink card and glue to the pop-up strips to create the effect of an iced cake. Use colourful card to die-cut ten small and six large candles using the Sizzix decorative die. Die cut just the tops of the candles from yellow card, glue in place and draw an orange swirl over the perforations with a felt-tip pen. Glue each candle onto the pop-up strips. From the deeper pink card cut two decorative edge strips and glue along the front and back edges.

✔ make a book
Create a simple pop-up album or storybook with your child by gluing three of four card pages together back to back.

kids' korner

Create a card blank from A4 (US letter) card. To get the maximum height for the pop-up, secure the pop-up strip so it is near the back of the card. Ask your child to draw the images on a piece of paper and cut them out. Hold the pop-up image against the strip and let it fall against the card, as it will when the card is closed. If the image protrudes from the card explain to your child that it needs to be shorter/narrower when drawn on card. Check the revised drawings, leave your child to colour them in, and then help secure them in place.

puzzle it out

Both intriguing and challenging, this card is a greeting and present in one. The recipient gets to assemble the puzzle themselves from the jigsaw pieces, which you pop in the envelope along with the card, and it will certainly surprise when the pieces spill out of the envelope. Double-sided tape on the card provides an area on which to place the assembled puzzle so that it can be saved as a card, or the pieces to can be assembled without the tape and used again and again.

The puzzle can be created on a ready-made jigsaw blank, like the birthday card opposite, or you can have all the fun of devising your own puzzle (see page 71). Either way, it can be decorated with freehand images, stamps or stencils, and you can make it as difficult or easy as you think the recipient can manage.

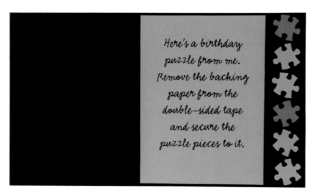

Here's a birthday puzzle from me. Remove the backing paper from the double-sided tape and secure the puzzle pieces to it.

Use the blue area inside the card to write your message and explain how to assemble the puzzle on the front.

This colourful 60th birthday card will stand out from the crowd when placed on the mantelpiece. One candle stamp has been used to create sixty candles, which presents another challenge – to count them all.

jigsaw card

Finished size 15cm (6in) square

See also
Making card blanks,
page 11
Stamping, page 22

you will need...

- Card maker's tool kit, page 8
- 26 x 15cm (10¼ x 6in) rectangle of black card
- Two 10.5 x 14.5cm (4⅛ x 5¾in) rectangles of bright blue card
- Scraps of blue, pink and orange card
- 10 x 14cm (4 x 5½) pre-cut puzzle blank
- Small puzzle punch
- Small candle rubber stamp
- Black permanent dye ink pad
- Permanent marker pens in bright colours, such as those by Galaxy

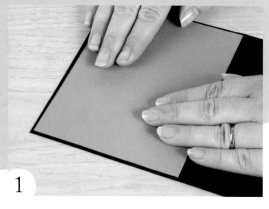

1

2

measure it

Make sure that the double-sided tape on the front of the card only extends as far as the puzzle edges. Otherwise the remainder will show once the puzzle has been stuck in place.

Lay out the black card. Measure 15cm (6in) across it and make a faint pencil guideline. Score and fold with the shorter side as the front. Using double-sided tape, glue a blue card rectangle inside the card near to the fold so that it can't be seen when the card is closed. Secure the other blue card rectangle to the front in the same way. This is the background for the puzzle.

Punch two orange, two pink and two blue puzzle shapes and glue them down the right-hand side of the card blank on the inside of the card, beside the blue card.

3

4

With the puzzle still intact, stamp it with candles. Use the black permanent ink, re-inking the stamp each time to get a crisp, clear image. Leave to dry completely. Now use permanent marker pens to add colour to your stamped design. (Avoid felt-tip pens because the colour may come off when the puzzle is handled.)

Provide an area of double-sided tape on the front blue card rectangle for the recipient to secure the puzzle pieces. Fix one row at the top, another at the bottom and two in-between. Do not remove the backing paper. On the inside blue rectangle write 'Here's a birthday puzzle from me. Remove the backing paper from the double-sided tape and secure the puzzle pieces to it.' Break up the puzzle pieces and place them with the card in an envelope.

further inspiration

See also
Making card blanks,
page 11

You don't have to use a pre-cut puzzle. Create your image on card and cut into puzzle pieces. Use straight or wavy lines to create large or small sections. If you prefer the traditional jigsaw design then try out the Coluzzle cutting system. It has a number of different puzzle design templates that you can place over your design to create a realistic puzzle.

party time This colourful children's birthday party invitation was created using computer clip art and then cut up into simple puzzle pieces.

Create a simple, colourful invitation on your computer and print it out onto thin card. Trim around the design and cut a piece of coloured card to the same size for the backing. Keeping in mind the age of the child recipient, use scissors to cut the puzzle into straight-sided puzzle pieces. Secure strips of double-sided tape, (in one direction only) down or across the backing card, ensuring that there is a strip of tape along each edge. Do not remove the backing paper from these strips. Write on the backing card: 'Remove the double-sided tape strips and complete this puzzle by sticking the puzzle pieces on this backing card'.

try this! Make the puzzle more complex for older children and adults by creating an intricate picture. Make it more puzzling by cutting the picture into small rectangles of a similar size. With these complex puzzles do ensure that you allow enough time for the puzzle to be completed before the party date.

bright ideas

- Buy a wooden puzzle base and send it in place of your greeting card. Decorate the puzzle, remembering to write on your greeting and then break it up and place it in a box. This novel puzzle is guaranteed to be assembled more than once.

- Base a child's treasure hunt around a collection of puzzle pieces. Draw a map showing where the treasure is buried and cut into a puzzle. Along with each treasure-hunt clue hide one piece of the puzzle. Only when all the pieces have been found can the puzzle be assembled to show where the treasure is hidden.

slide and pull

Lift the lid on this card to reveal the surprise within. Anything could pop up when you do so, from the friendly teddy face shown opposite to a family photograph or even a spooky Halloween ghost. Die-cut images, like the teddy face, make the process really easy, but you can have a lot of fun devising your own pull-ups (see page 77).

Making this card is wonderfully straightforward once you understand its construction. The item to be revealed, such as the bear's head, is stuck to the top of a strip of card that will act as a stopper. This is then sealed between two pieces of card with a gap at the top that is wide enough for the head to pass through but too narrow for the stopper. The 'lid' is stuck to the top of the head. When you lift the lid the head pops up out of the card pocket but the stopper prevents it from being pulled right out – simple.

This card opens up just like any other, but if you lift the lid there's a delightful surprise in store.

This card is perfect for teddy bear lovers and collectors of all ages because hidden inside is a teddy just waiting to say hello. Wrapping ribbon around the finished card gives the realistic appearance of a gift box.

teddy bear card

Finished size 15 x 13cm (6 x 5⅛in)

you will need...

- Card maker's tool kit, page 8

- Mustard card: 15 x 13cm (6 x 5⅛in) folded card blank; 15 x 10cm (6 x 4in) rectangle; 15 x 4cm (6 x 1½in) strip; 15cm (6in) square

- Decorative paper: 15 x 10cm (6 x 4in) rectangle; 15 x 4cm (6 x 1½in) strip; 14 x 2.5cm (5½ x 1in) strip

- Teddy bear face die cut

- 40 (16in) of 2cm (¾in) wide blue ribbon

See also
Making card blanks, page 11
Strengthening papers, page 16

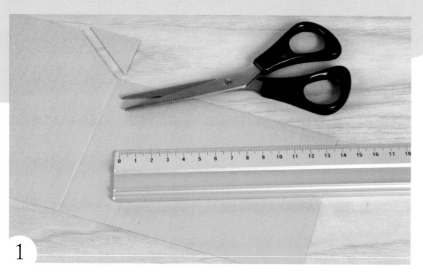

1

Measure 3cm (1³⁄₁₆in) down the back of the card blank and draw a guideline across the back. Cut along the line and then up the fold to remove the excess card. Along the top of the front measure 3.5cm (1³⁄₈in) from the fold. Draw a guideline from this point to the fold and remove this triangle with scissors, as shown in the photograph.

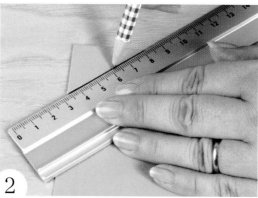

2

Flip the triangle over and place over the other top back corner. Lay your ruler against it, remove the triangle and draw in a guideline on the card back. Cut off this triangle too.

3

Glue the 15 x 10cm (6 x 4in) paper rectangle onto the card rectangle of the same size. Turn over and, keeping as near to the edge as possible, apply 5mm (³⁄₁₆in) double-sided tape along the bottom and up both sides. Measure 2cm (¾in) in from each top corner and apply pieces of double-sided tape here too. To help secure the ribbon add a further 1.5cm (⁵⁄₈in) of tape centrally at the bottom.

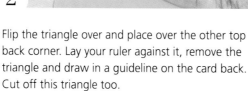

4

Trim the white border from around the bear's face and glue the bear centrally onto the square of mustard card. Find the centre bottom of the face and measure 6.5cm (2⁹/₁₆in) out to each side. Measure 1cm (³/₈in) above and below this line. This is to create a stopper at the bottom of the face.

5

Cut around the bear's face and stopper. Check that it fits between the tape on the mustard rectangle. Now check that the gap between the tape at the top is wide enough for the face to pass through but not the stopper, as shown.

right height

When making your own version of the slide and pull card, make sure that the height of the face and stopper are no taller than the space between the top and bottom of the rectangle. Remember also to take into account the width of the double-sided tape.

stopper width

Check your stopper width before you glue the layers together. To allow easy movement of the pull-up the stopper must be a little narrower than the width between the double-sided tape yet wider than the gap left at the top of the box.

teddy bear card

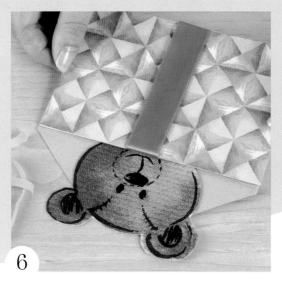

6

7

Remove the backing paper from the tape along the bottom of the rectangle. Cut 20cm (8in) of ribbon and wrap it centrally around the rectangle you have been working on, keeping the join on the inside and at the bottom. Lay the bear and stopper on the card blank, removing the remaining backing paper from the tape and secure the rectangle on top of the card blank, trapping the bear and stopper inside.

Create the box lid by gluing the 4cm (1½in) wide paper strip onto the matching card strip. Turn over and measure 1cm (³⁄₈in) up from the bottom and draw a guideline. Wrap the remainder of the ribbon around the lid, tie in a bow and trim the ends. Lay the box lid on top of the face to decide where to secure it.

secure ribbon

Ensure that the ribbon is firmly secured at both ends. This is important because the pull-up may catch on any ribbon sticking out from the card, hampering its movement.

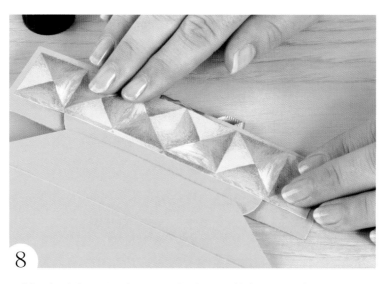

8

Holding both layers in place, turn the face and lid over. Apply glue above the guideline to stick the face to the lid. (Not gluing below the line enables the box lid to overlap the box, giving a realistic appearance.) Glue the thin strip of paper over the join. Write inside: 'Can you reveal my surprise? Just lift up the box lid.'

further inspiration

See also
Making card blanks,
page 11

There are a variety of ways to alter the appearance of this card. The easiest way to make a difference is to change the size and papers used for the card. Decorate it with wrapping paper, brown paper stamped with images, leftover wallpaper, advertisements or pictures cut from comics. Change the shape from a gift box to a teapot, hat box, sweetie jar or even a television.

striped sensation
The gold striped card and trimmings give this card a sophisticated feel. It's an ideal way of preserving and displaying an important family photograph.

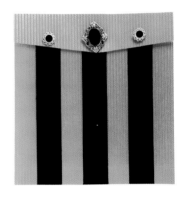

Glue 2cm (¾in) black velvet ribbon at equal intervals onto a 15cm (6in) gold card square. Cut a box lid 4cm (1½in) deep, taper the lower edges and glue on three fancy buttons. Glue the photograph onto black card that is slightly wider all round and add the stopper at the base. Cut out and assemble on a 15cm (6in) card blank as for the teddy bear, omitting the triangles that create the illusion of a box. Fix the box lid in place.

try this!

Make this card for a birthday, enclosing the age of the recipient made from die cuts. This is ideal for the bashful because their age is not displayed unless the lid is lifted.

bright ideas

- Cut out photos from a catalogue of the presents it would be nice to get at Christmas. Glue these onto the pull-up, make a card shaped like a sack and send it to Santa.
- Create a simple house shape from coloured card with a roof that lifts to reveal details of a housewarming party.
- For a magic lover, send birthday greetings in the shape of a top hat so that pulling up the rim lifts a rabbit out the hat.

lift the flaps

The excitement created by lift-the-flaps books makes the idea perfect for translation into a novelty card. Kids love them firstly because of the surprise of what lies underneath the flaps, and later for the anticipation of what they know to be there. Adults can love them for the same reason as well as the resonances with their own childhoods.

The flaps in this book are easily made simply by placing five mini cards inside a larger one, so you don't have to worry about cutting complicated apertures. It's the perfect base to celebrate an event such as an anniversary because it gives you the opportunity to include seven images, all from different key events, but it could be used for any purpose – key events in a life for a birthday card, each family member in a Christmas card and so on. You can even omit the photos and create something altogether different, see pages 82–83.

2001

Untie the ribbon to reveal a lifetime of memories...

This 50th wedding anniversary card doubles as a mini scrapbook, making it a wonderful keepsake. The large outer card acts as the album cover and is tied closed with ribbon. Inside there are five mini cards in varying sizes. As each one is opened a photo from a memorable event is revealed.

journey through time

Finished size 14 x 20cm (5½ x 8in)

you will need...

○ Card maker's tool kit, page 8

○ 10 x 15cm (4 x 6in) main portrait photo (A1)

○ Three 5 x 7.5cm (2 x 3in) landscape photos (A2, C and D)

○ Three 7.5 x 5cm (3 x 2in) portrait photos (B, E and F)

○ Cream textured folded mini card blanks:
14 x 20cm (5½ x 8in) main card A;
14 x 13cm (5½ x 5⅛in) card B;
12 x 13cm (4¾ x 5⅛in) card C;
11 x 12cm (4⅜ x 4¾in) card D;
11 x 10cm (4⅜ x 4in) card E;
9 x 10cm (3½ x 4in) front-opening card F

○ Selection of coordinating scrapbook papers:
12.5 x 20cm (5 x 8in) paper A1 (front);
12.5 x 20cm (5 x 8in) paper A2; 12 x 13cm (4¾ x 5⅛in) paper B;
11 x 12cm (4⅜ x 4¾in) paper C; 10 x 11cm (4 x 4⅜in) paper D;
10 x 9cm (4 x 3⅝in) paper E; 8 x 9cm (3⅛ x 3⅝in) paper F

○ Six 8.5 x 6cm (3⅜ x 2⅜in) photo mats of coordinating scrapbook papers

○ 90cm (1yd) of 1.5cm (¾in) wide sheer cream ribbon

○ A4 (US letter) cream card

○ Xyron and permanent adhesive

○ Computer and colour printer

See also
Making card blanks,
page 11

printer perfect

Before printing anything onto card, like the dates used here, print out onto ordinary copier paper. Make any adjustments needed and only when you are completely happy print onto your card.

1

Type the dates of each event on your computer in appropriate colours and fonts. Make the date for the main photo (A1) larger than the others. Print out onto A4 cream card. Cut out the main date in a tight rectangle; cut the rest out as a block. Apply adhesive to the six small photographs, scrapbook papers and dates by running them through a Xyron machine. Remove the Xyron top film and trim each date into a rectangle. Secure paper A1 to the centre front of card A. Fold the ribbon in half, crease, open up and lay the ribbon halfway down, across the front with the ribbon crease on the card fold. Hold in place with a little glue until properly secured under a photo. Use sticky fixer pads to add photo A1 and its date.

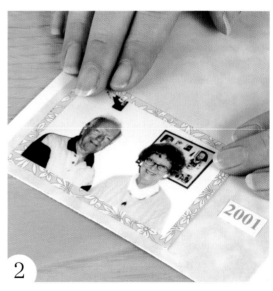

2

Open the main card and stick paper A2 in place. Secure the photo A2 on a coordinating paper mat and then on the bottom left-hand corner of the card. Secure the date beside it.

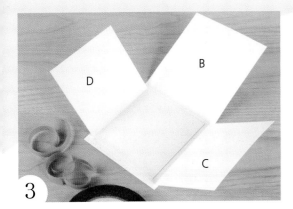

3

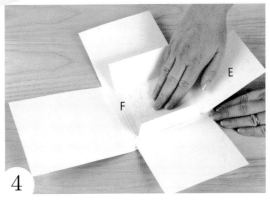

4

Lay the mini card blanks one on top of the other, starting with the largest, (B), with the fold across the top. Secure card C next with the fold on the right and card D over that with the fold on the left. Secure each card centrally with double-sided tape.

Continue in the same way, securing card E with the fold at the bottom. Finally in the middle secure the front opening card F.

5

6

on track

To avoid confusion, label each card and photo on the back in pencil where it will eventually be stuck down.

Close each mini card, starting with the smallest and then attach the card stack to the large card with double-sided tape with the top fold just below the top edge of the main card.

Now open up all the mini cards and stick the backing papers, photo mats, photographs and dates on each one. Treat each card separately.

its a wrap

If desired, you can incorporate a tie to keep the front opening mini card (F) closed by trapping a length of narrow ribbon underneath it as it is secured in place.

7

When complete, close each card one by one, starting with the smallest and shut the card. Use the ribbon under photo A1 to wrap around the card and finish with a neat bow.

further inspiration

This idea is easily adaptable. Change the number and size of the mini cards and alternate the folds in different ways to change the overall appearance. You can also reverse the idea completely and instead of securing the mini cards inside the main one add one, two or three to the card front. Make a feature of this by decorating the front of the outer mini card and then tie it closed with a length of ribbon.

See also
Strengthening papers,
page 16
Using craft punches,
page 20

silent night This card depicts the true meaning of Christmas with a three-dimensional stable and raffia for the straw. The starry sky is created with Sizzix paddle punches.

Make a front-opening 15cm (6in) square card blank from double-sided gold card. Strengthen patterned paper for the roof and sides by sticking it to card. The stable roof is a top-folded mini card 11 x 12cm (4¼ x 4¾in); the stable sides are constructed from a 10 x 26cm (4 x 10¼in) rectangle that is scored and folded 8cm (3⅛in) in from each side. Use the template on page 110 to make two dark brown mangers, cut one out and glue short strips of raffia on top. Cut out the top section of the second manger and trim it into three strips. Glue these strips on top of the manger and then glue the manger onto the stable. Add more raffia coming out from the manger and on the floor of the stable. Punch a small circle from gold parchment and add gold glitter around the edge. Glue above the manger. Use Sizzix paddle punches to cut out the stars and then tie the card closed with raffia.

try this! Turn the stable into a cosy room with a roaring fire for a new home greeting. Alternatively, use pretty vellums to create a beautiful greenhouse filled with flowers and good wishes for a gardening enthusiast.

bright ideas

• Create an amazing card for an older child by using photos taken of them each year.

• Write wedding details on the small mini card in the centre and give each member of the family one mini card to decorate with a special photo and their hand-written sentiments for a wedding card to treasure.

bright ideas

- Use this idea to get extra space on your scrapbook pages.
- Make your own story-book greeting card by using each mini card as a different chapter. Your story could include the recipient or familiar places with small drawings and stickers as illustrations.

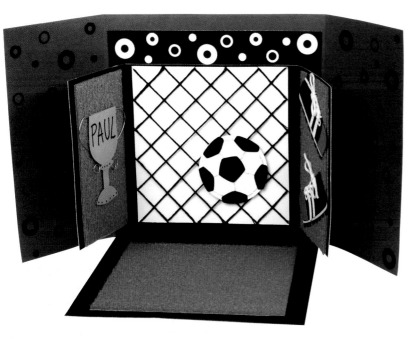

football crazy Celebrate football (soccer) with this funky soccer card. Green flannel paper provides the soft texture of grass while black embroidery cotton (floss) and white card create a football net. Three-dimensional stickers and peel-off eyelets add to the decoration.

Make a front opening 14cm (5½in) red square card blank. From black card create a bottom-folded mini card 13.5cm (5⅛in) square and a 10 x 11cm (4 x 4¼in) front-opening one. Construct a net by winding black embroidery cotton (floss) around a 10cm (4in) white square of card. This is made easier if you cut small notches at each corner and at 2cm (¾in) intervals around the edges. Write your recipient's name on the gold cup and then secure the green flannel paper, the net and ready-made three-dimensional football stickers. Create a graphic illusion of a crowd and footballs by using black-and-white circular eyelet peel-offs. Add further decoration to the front and tie closed with football laces.

try this! Make the card in team colours or change the sport to golf, basketball, baseball or fishing. For someone who prefers a stroll and a picnic, use checked paper to suggest a tablecloth and stickers to create a teddy-bears picnic.

✓ **rainy day**
On a rainy day supply card, art items and old magazines for cutting up. Encourage your children to create their own books full of jokes, puzzles, funny poems and drawings.

kids' korner

When asked to decorate a greeting card, many children find that there just isn't enough space. This certainly isn't a problem here. Create the large and mini cards with your child and secure in place. Keep it colourful by using different colours for each card – you could use the colours of the rainbow; red, orange, yellow, green, blue, indigo and violet. Close each card and then add numbers to the front of each one. Now the order in which the cards are opened and shut is obvious and your child can get on with the fun task of adding the decorations.

mobile magic

Like a mini mobile, a decorative shape dangles in the aperture of this card, moving gently with the breeze to draw the eye and bring a smile to the face. The dangle and its aperture can be any shape you like and the card can also be cut into unusual designs, as in the blue Easter card opposite or the Halloween card on page 88. In fact, you can modify this card as much as you like. Even the dangle can be changed – try using buttons or shapes made from modelling clay, for example.

This card may look complex but it is very easy to construct. Remember when you were a child making a Christmas tree by slotting two pieces of card together, one with a slit in the top and the other with a slit in the bottom? This card is constructed using the same principle. In this instance two card blanks with apertures are used and, by feeding one card through the aperture in the other, you can create a three-dimensional space for the dangle to hang in. This makes this dangle card very different from the traditional two-sided aperture card.

These Easter cards show how effective a dangle card can be. The yellow one has patterned paper decorations made into stickers, some of which have been modified for a three-dimensional effect. The purple one is basically the same but it has a decoration of six diamond-shaped quilt blocks and the card has been trimmed away around these to create zigzag edges.

easter eggstravaganza!

Finished size 11 x 20cm (4⅜ x 8in)

you will need...

- ○ Card maker's tool kit, page 8
- ○ Two 11 x 20cm (4⅜ x 8in) yellow folded card blanks
- ○ A4 (US letter) sheet of white card
- ○ A4 (US letter) sheet of purple card
- ○ Square craft punch

- ○ Quilt-pattern paper
- ○ Lemon yellow thread
- ○ Xyron machine with permanent cartridge or spray adhesive
- ○ Small hole punch

See also
Making card blanks, page 11
Using templates, page 25
Using craft punches, page 20
Making and customizing stickers, page 18
Strengthening papers, page 16

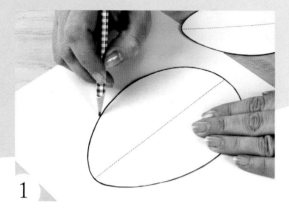

1

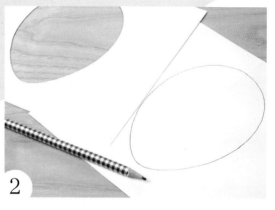

2

accurate apertures

Placing the first card blank over the second and tracing through the aperture is a virtually foolproof way of ensuring that both apertures will meet at top and bottom. You can also draw freehand apertures using this method.

Make a white card template from each of the egg-shaped patterns on page 110. Take one lemon card blank and open it out. Place the larger egg template in the middle, 2.5cm (1in) from the bottom, and ensure that it is central by lining up the centre line on the template with the centre fold. Use a pencil to trace around the template and then cut it out as an aperture.

Place the first card blank on top of the second card blank and align all sides. Lightly trace through the aperture onto the second card blank with a pencil. Cut out and erase any pencil marks around the apertures.

3

4

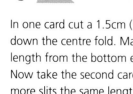

In one card cut a 1.5cm (⅝in) slit from the top edge down the centre fold. Make a second slit the same length from the bottom edge along the centre fold. Now take the second card blank and make two more slits the same length, again along the centre fold, but this time from inside the aperture, as shown here.

Take the card blank with the slits on the outside and bend it gently so that it is not quite folded in half. Feed this card into the aperture on the second card blank. Manoeuvre both card blanks so that the slits at the bottom slot into each other. Repeat so that the top slits slot into each other too.

86 mobile magic

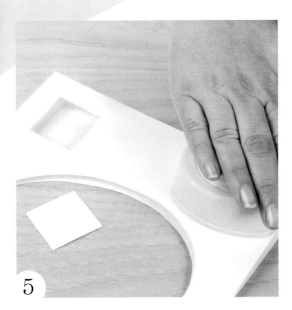

5

To create the windows on the front right-hand side, feed the top card into the craft punch. Line up the punch with the top edge and punch out a window. Slide the punch down and make another window near the bottom edge. Punch a third window in the middle on the left-hand side.

6

To make the decorative stickers roughly cut out pictures from the patterned paper, apply adhesive by running these through a Xyron machine and then cut out accurately. Attach your stickers. (I stuck the sun directly onto the card blank but turned the butterflies and pots of flowers into part-relief stickers so that the flowers and wings stand up. I strengthened the rabbits and then pressed one behind each window.) Finally, lay the card flat and secure a quilt block behind each window on the card underneath.

hanging options

You don't have to use thread to hang your dangle. Try using wire to create a stationary dangle or fine ribbon to create a swing in a rectangular aperture.

7

Create the egg-shaped dangle by cutting a piece of quilt paper slightly larger than the small egg template and add stability to it by gluing it to the purple card. Place the small egg template on top and trace around it with a pencil. Cut the egg out and punch a small hole at the top. Feed the lemon thread through this hole and arrange the dangle in the aperture so that you can gauge where it should hang.

8

Secure the dangle by taking the threads through the slits, tying in a knot and then trimming the ends. Move the knot so that it is hidden behind a slit.

further inspiration

The two variations here show how the dangle card can be adapted to suit any number of different occasions from Halloween to the birth of a new baby. Although I usually make my dangle cards so that they have an obvious four-sided front view, you can adapt this design by decorating the backs too. If you do this, remember that the card will be viewed from all angles so you need to think about the decoration carefully (see carousel caper, page 38).

halloween pumpkin
Made from orange card with black bat buttons, this card is huge fun. If you can't get the buttons, make your own bats from modelling clay or black card.

Make two folded cards from heavyweight orange card, then use the pumpkin template on page 110 to cut them both to shape. Cut out oval apertures then make the slits and assemble the card in the same way as the Easter card (see page 86). On the front facing sides draw the curved lines using a black felt-tip pen. Hang two bat buttons glued together in the aperture and decorate each front facing side with two bat buttons.

 try this! Adapt this card by creating a haunted house shape and decorating it with spooky ghosts, spiders and tombstones.

slit length

To calculate the length of each slit measure the distance from the outside edge to the aperture and then divide by two. Cut each slit so that the length is a little more than this measurement.

 bright ideas
• For a soccer, tennis or baseball fan make a ball-shaped dangle card, (trimmed flat at the bottom so that it will stand), and hang a gold cup or trophy in the aperture. Decorate the sides with items from the game, such as boots, bats, nets and final scores.
• To make your dangle card into a gift, hang a key ring, funky bracelet or birthday badge in the aperture.

bright ideas

- Draw attention to a special birthday or anniversary by hanging a sparkly die-cut number in the aperture.
- For a truly coordinated look create your dangle card using pictures cut from the same paper that you will use to wrap your gift.

fine tuning

If the card join is too tight or stiff then the card may not stand up properly. To rectify this use scissors to remove a fine slither of card from one of the slits at the bottom and another at the top.

new baby This card is made in the same way as the Easter card but with a rectangular aperture. The decorations are clear stickers, which blend subtly into the background.

Make two blue speckled card blanks and cut out rectangular apertures nearer to the top than the bottom. Cut slits and assemble in the same way as the Easter card (see page 86). Remove 2.5cm (1in) from the front left- and right-hand sides to make the front cards narrower and show more of the back cards. Decorate all front facing sides using clear stickers. Make an oval dangle and decorate with a clear sticker too.

try this! You can adapt this card by hanging a photo of the baby, a die-cut silver spoon, or tiny handmade felt baby shoes in the aperture.

kids' orner

Children will love decorating the many faces of this card with stickers, stamps and so on. One idea is to help them make thank-you cards decorated with pictures cut from the wrapping paper that their gifts were wrapped in. Help them to measure and cut the pieces as necessary, then assemble and mark with a small pencil cross any sides that are to be left undecorated. Turn the wrapping paper designs into stickers and then leave your child to decorate the card and dangle. Erase the pencil crosses and secure the dangle in place.

rattle 'n' shake

The first thing many of us do when we receive a present is to give it a little shake and see what kind of noise it makes. If you know someone else like that, they'll love this intriguing card, which gives a pleasing sound when rattled. The secret is in the foam box frame with a clear acetate window that is fixed to the front of the card. Slip your 'shakeables' inside, and the recipient can see them fly about and hear that satisfying shaking sound.

Exactly what sound your card makes all depends on what's in it. See what you already have about the house. Sequins, beads, glitter, punched shapes, seeds, small buttons, confetti, little pasta shapes, rock salts and other coarse spices are all excellent, or you may come up with your own ideas. The filling may even be the inspiration for the whole card. Copy the card shown here or design your own. Pages 94–95 show four variations and provide plenty of other ideas to get you started.

This shaker card has a practical theme that would suit any home-improvement enthusiast and make a special thank you card for someone who has helped you with his or her do-it-yourself skills. The box is filed with a mixture of real washers and silver card washers. All the other 'tools' are ready-made stickers and relief stickers.

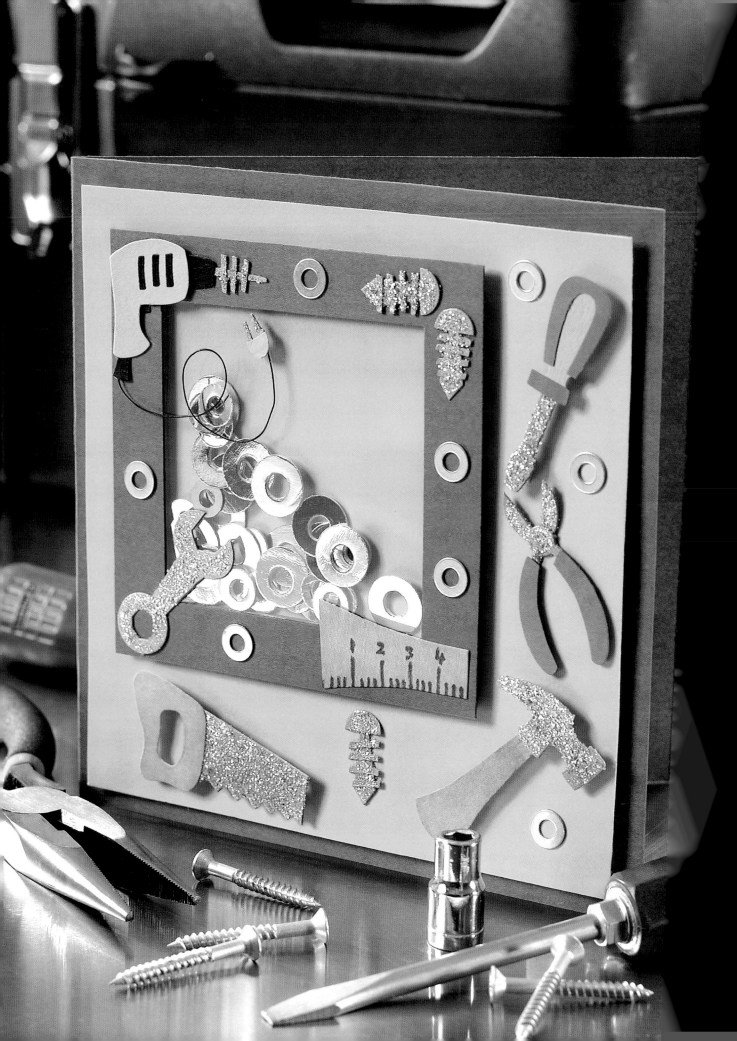

home improvements

Finished size 15cm (6in) square

you will need...

○ Card maker's tool kit, page 8

○ 15cm (6in) folded square red card blank

○ 14cm (5½in) square of yellow card

○ 9cm (3½in) square of red card

○ 8.5cm (3⅜in) square of red self-adhesive foam

○ 8.5cm (3⅜in) square of acetate

○ A5 (8 x 6in) sheet of shiny silver card

○ Circle craft punches – 12mm (½in) and 8mm (⅜in)

○ 4mm (⅛in) and 8mm (⅜in) hole punches

○ Craft hammer

○ DIY-theme stickers

○ Fine silver glitter

○ Roughly 12 small silver metal washers

Note: You can use foam that is not self-adhesive but ordinary UPVA glue will not secure acetate to it. Run the foam through a Xyron machine (permanent adhesive), prior to cutting out the aperture.

See also
Making card blanks, page 11
Cutting apertures, page 12
Making and customizing stickers, page 18
Enhancing stickers, page 19

1

cutting accuracy

For speed, ease and accuracy use a die cutting machine or shape cutting system to remove the apertures.

Cut a 6.5cm (2½in) aperture centrally in both the small square of red card and the square of red self-adhesive foam. Glue the square yellow card to the front of the red card blank for the background.

2

Calculate where to place your shaker box by measuring 1.5cm (⅝in) from the top and folded edges of the card blank and mark lightly with the pencil. Apply a thin layer of glue over the non-adhesive side of the red foam frame and secure it to the card blank, lining it up with the pencil guidelines. Do not remove the backing paper from the foam yet.

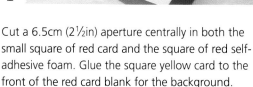

3

Use the brush to apply glue thinly over the wrong side of the card frame and press the acetate on top. Remove any excess prior to sticking to prevent glue oozing out onto the acetate window. Allow to dry.

handling acetate

Always try to hold acetate by the edges to avoid getting your fingerprints on the surface. Use a soft cloth to remove any marks.

problems with static

When using items that may cling to the acetate, such as sequins or small beads, wipe over the underside of the acetate with an antistatic polishing cloth before you glue it in place. This will help eliminate the problem.

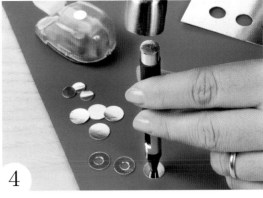

4

Punch out about fifteen 8mm (³⁄₈in) and fifteen 12mm (½in) circles of silver card. Use the 4mm (¹⁄₈in) hole punch to remove the centres from all the smaller circles and the 8mm (³⁄₈in) hole punch to remove the centres from all the larger ones. Add all these washers to the shaker well, ensuring that the silver side is uppermost. Add four metal washers to create a little noise when shaken.

5

Peel the backing paper from the foam frame and press the acetate shaker window on top, trapping all the washers inside.

6

Enliven your stickers by gluing glitter to all the silver parts. Allow to dry.

7

For added dimension, turn the saw, hammer and screwdriver into relief stickers. Use the tweezers to hold each sticker and then fit in place with sticky fixer pads.

8

Remove the remaining stickers from the sheet one by one with the tweezers and press onto the card. Add further interest to the design by gluing on eight metal washers.

further inspiration

You can decorate your shaker card in lots of different ways to give it totally new looks. Stamping is an excellent means of decoration – it's quick, gives good results, and there are masses of lovely designs to choose from. I suggest that you use the shaker items as your starting point and build your design and colour scheme around these. However, do be sure that your shaker items are not so heavy that they will cause the card to topple over.

See also
Stamping, page 22
Using craft punches, page 20
Beads, sequins and charms, page 24
Heat embossing, page 23

sunflower birthday
Sunflower seeds make a good, solid sound when rattled. Combine with stamped designs for a delightfully quick and easy shaker card.

Make a folded square brown card blank and glue a smaller orange square to the front. For the shaker box cut a round aperture from a brown square of card and use brown dye ink to create a subtle background of rubber-stamped sunflower heads. Make up the shaker, filling it with sunflower seeds from a multi-seed pack and then mount onto the card blank. Stamp more sunflower heads onto yellow card with black waterproof dye ink and add plenty of colour with marker pens. Cut these out and fix to the shaker with sticky fixer pads.

 try this! Put seeds in your shaker and provide sowing and growing instructions so the recipient can use them in their own garden.

snowman christmas
Rock salt and fine glitter ensure a white Christmas. Rubber-stamp snowmen and snowflakes, and glitter glue make decorating the card a breeze.

Make a folded square lilac card blank. Cut a round aperture from a white square of card and create a background of lilac rubber-stamped snowflakes, using a lilac brush marker to ink up the stamp. Add sparkle between the snowflakes with dots of glitter glue. Use a pencil to trace lightly through the aperture onto white background card. Stamp snowmen within the pencilled circle using black waterproof dye ink, and colour with pastel marker pens. Make up the shaker, filling it with rock salt and fine glitter, and then mount it onto the card blank.

 try this! For a fun summer themed card, fill the shaker with play sand, or mini shells collected from a beach holiday.

 **bright ideas**
• For a child's birthday turn comic-book pictures into stickers and use these to decorate the card.
• If you have a fisherman or sailor in the family, turn your shaker well into a fish bowl or porthole.

baby girl

This personalized card is stamped with pink dye, though you could change it to blue for a boy. The letters of the child's name hang from threads to add movement.

Make a tall folded white card blank and rubber-stamp a background of baby images and letters. Cut a square aperture from a white square of card and dab with the same pink. Randomly attach small white seed beads. Rubber stamp the child's name twice onto white card and use a craft punch to cut these letters into squares. Give the letters definition by outlining with a pink gel pen. Thread more white beads onto white thread and trap the thread by gluing two letter squares together. Make up the shaker, filling it with a mix of white and pink seed beads. Trap the beaded threads between the acetate and foam.

 Decorate the frame with small buttons instead of beads and use alphabet beads to spell out the child's name.

golden wedding

For a special event, such as a wedding, gold filigree and embossed stamping add refinement. Gold card, beads and sequins complete the look.

Make a large gold card blank. Cut a rectangular aperture from a rectangle of gold card. Using gold thread and a needle sew the gold filigree corner embellishments around the aperture and to the corners of the card blank. Use a pencil to trace lightly through the aperture onto cream background card. Stamp and emboss a wedding cake in gold on the card within the pencilled frame. Make up the shaker, filling it with a mix of gold hole-less beads and small gold heart sequins, and then mount onto the card blank.

 Instead of filigree corners you could use gold doilies. Try changing the colours for a unique silver or ruby wedding anniversary card.

child care
If you are making a card for a young child, don't tempt them with brightly coloured shaker items that they might try to reach and eat. Instead use coloured sand.

kids' korner

Children will love this card, and I am sure that they will come up with lots of (un)suitable ideas for items to shake! A nice idea is to ask your child to draw a freehand shape for the shaker frame onto card and cut it out. Use a ballpoint pen to trace around it and through the aperture onto the foam and cut out (a pencil will not work on foam). You can then create an original-shaped shaker box.

surprise, surprise!

The surprise paper insert in this card explodes like an unfurling flower as it is opened, and the flat card is transformed into a three-dimensional masterpiece. As an added surprise, you can fill the space inside the insert with small items such as confetti, sequins or chocolates, making this a card and gift in one.

A folded insert card is much more straightforward to make than it looks, requiring just a few basic folds, though I suggest that you practice these on scrap paper before you begin. The wedding card, shown opposite, and the handbag card on page 102 have flaps to secure any items you wish to slip inside, and this also provides an area on which to write your message. If desired you can make a simpler card to be used without a filling that doesn't have a flap, like the angel greetings card on page 103.

Eye-catching decorations added to the front of the card create a good first impression, and help to ensure that the recipient opens it the right way up.

I made this wedding card using blue and white as a move away from traditional wedding colours. The blue of the sponge-effect card combines well with the white folded insert and glitter stickers. Before tying the card closed, small sequins can be dropped inside to add a final touch of magic when the card is first opened.

wedding toast

Finished size 11 x 15cm (4¾ x 6in)

See also
Making and customizing
stickers, page 18
Making card blanks,
page 11
Enhancing stickers,
page 19

you will need…

- ○ Card maker's tool kit, page 8
- ○ 15 x 30cm (6 x 12in) and 13 x 6cm (5⅛ x 2⅜in) rectangles of blue and white sponge-effect card
- ○ 20cm (8in) square and 13 x 6cm (5⅛ x 2⅜in) rectangle of good-quality white paper
- ○ Wedding theme stickers (purchased or made yourself)
- ○ Fine holographic glitter
- ○ 1 meter (1 yard) of gold ribbon

look sharp

Crisp, accurate folds will not only give a more polished result, but will make construction much easier too.

1

Fold the white paper square from corner to corner and use the bone folder to crease along the fold. Open out the paper.

2

Fold the paper again, this time matching the other two corners and use the bone folder to crease along the fold. Open out the paper again.

3

Turn the paper square over and fold the bottom edge up to the top. Use the bone folder to crease along the fold and then open the paper back out.

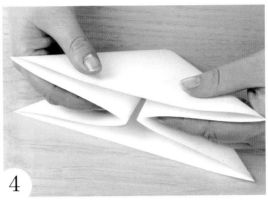

4

Turn the paper square back over again, place it on a flat surface and gently push the two sides inwards. (They will automatically fold in this way if your folds are firm and crisp.)

fancy that

For an ornate touch, give the insert fancy edges by trimming with decorative scissors once the folds have been made.

5

Fold one top outer corner to the centre and crease well with the bone folder. Repeat for the other top corner, as shown.

new look

For an alternative look, omit the four small final folds of the explosion.

6

Open up the explosion a little and tuck in the points you have just folded. Provided that you have creased the folds well this will be easy. Turn the explosion over and repeat steps 5 and 6; put to one side.

wedding toast

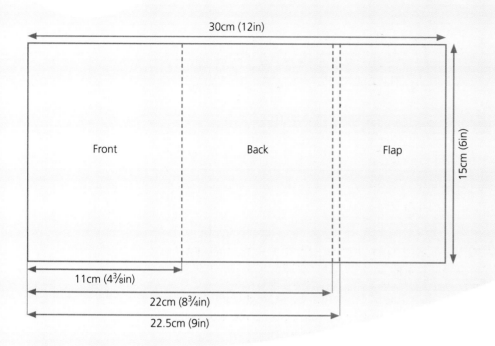

30cm (12in)

Front

Back

Flap

15cm (6in)

11cm (4³⁄₈in)

22cm (8³⁄₄in)

22.5cm (9in)

7

8

Use a pencil and ruler to make two faint guidelines 11cm (4³⁄₈in) and 22cm (8³⁄₄in) in from one short edge of the large sponge-effect rectangle of card, as shown in the diagram, above. Score with the ruler and stylus and then crease along both guidelines with the bone folder. To allow for the depth of the explosion insert also measure, score and fold 22.5cm (9in) from the same edge.

Glue the rectangle of white paper onto the card flap for your message. Apply double-sided tape along the top and bottom edges of the explosion. Remove the backing paper from the tape on the bottom edge and, with the point facing towards the 11cm (4³⁄₈in) fold, secure the explosion centrally, lining it up along the 22cm (8³⁄₄in) fold. Keep the explosion flat, remove the remaining backing paper and fold the top of the card blank over, trapping the explosion inside. Note that the point of the explosion will be about 1cm (³⁄₈in) away from the 11cm (4³⁄₈in) fold. This ensures that when the card is open its own weight does not cause the explosion to close it back down.

9

Remove any of the stickers not being used from the sheet to avoid getting glitter on them. Now add sparkle to the remaining stickers with glitter. Also add a fine line of glitter along the folds of the explosion and around the white message card on the flap. Allow to dry.

10

Remove the glittered stickers from the sheet with tweezers and arrange them on the explosion, the message card and the small sponge-effect card, which will form the front of the card when closed. To give an effect of champagne bubbles around the glasses add small dots of glitter.

11

Turn the card over and glue the ribbon centrally to the outside of the flap. This will be covered by the decorated card front.

open
this way

Check that you have placed the decorations on the front of the card the correct way round, as these reveal which way up the card should be opened.

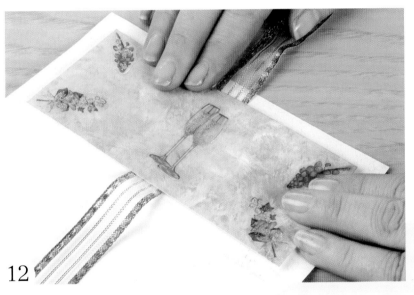

12

Apply sticky fixer pads along the edges of the back of the decorated card. Press the card centrally onto the outside flap so that it also covers the glue holding the ribbon in place. Place a handful of sequins into the explosion, then close by folding the flap over and tying the ribbon in a neat bow. Trim the ribbon ends.

further inspiration

The explosion insert is very versatile as these two variations show. The flower handbag card turns the explosion onto its end by creating a pocket that will hold small items. The angel greetings card is a more simplified version of my wedding card that omits the flap. The scope for making this card is limitless and the variety of materials that you can use is endless. I am sure that each of you will come up with beautiful and unique explosion cards.

See also
Using templates,
page 25

flower power This clever card doubles as a gift bag for small items such as an invitation, voucher or chocolate coins. It is simple to make using the template provided.

Use the template on page 109 to cut the handbag shape from pink pearlized card. Make two cuts in the top fold, feed through ribbon to create a handle and secure on the inside back with adhesive. Create an insert by folding a 20cm (8in) square of cerise paper into an explosion and then secure inside, covering up the ends of the ribbon. Decorate the outside with readymade beaded flower stickers and add a small hook-and-loop (Velcro) fastening under the flap.

try this! Turn the handbag card into a sports' bag card. Decorate it with stickers and rubber-stamped images that reflect the recipient's favourite sport.

bright ideas
- Make a suitcase-shape card with a buckle fastening and decorate with used postage stamps to say bon voyage to a friend. Pop in some miniature photos of you all together.
- Use a few sprigs of dried lavender in the decoration and when the celebration has passed your card can be used as a sachet to scent linen and clothes.

angelic greetings
Send a message of love or understanding, decorated with pretty stickers and a punch. This version does not have a pocket that you can fill.

Make a folded dusky pink A5 (8 x 6in) card with an explosion insert from fine striped paper. Use a craft punch to decorate the folds and then secure the explosion inside the card. Add two strips of coordinating paper down each side. Decorate with clear angel stickers, add pink ribbon and tie closed.

 try this! The explosion fold is wonderful for scrapbook journaling. When closed it takes up very little space and yet provides a large area when open.

finding inspiration

If you are stuck for a design, look through your collections of stickers, stamps, punches and other craft materials. Dig out those half-forgotten items that you bought on a whim and never used, and build your card design around them.

 ✓

party time
Set up a production line with your child to make simple explosion cards for their birthday party. Fill with sweets and give to the guests as they leave.

kids' korner

The name of this card will excite children straight away and conjure up all sorts of ideas. You will probably need to make the explosion insert and assemble the card, but you can leave them to decorate it, making sure they know not to place stickers over the folds. Instead of ribbon try using string, garden twine, raffia or wool for your tie and instead of securing your tie to the card with glue keep it closed by just tying it in a bow around the card.

starburst

With so many people making their own cards these days, you have to go one step further to make yours stand out from the crowd. This beautiful three-dimensional card does just that. It looks like a highly complicated piece of origami, but it's actually made in sections that are glued together. Just fold five squares of paper in three easy folds then glue them together, adding two outer covers, a length of ribbon and some beads. It's wonderfully satisfying when you open out your card for the first time and see the beautiful star you have created.

You can make your star look as extravagant as you like. The Christmas starburst card uses punched shapes to decorate the plain side of the paper. The advantage of this is that once you have purchased your punch, the shapes are virtually free. However, you could equally well use stamped designs, stencilled images, stickers or even simple drawn lines or squiggles. For a really ornate look, glue on beaded cord and peel-offs, as for the wedding card on page 108.

The hanging star card will arrive closed, like this. To open, slide both beads away from it and open out. Create a clever loop for hanging by sliding one bead back to the card.

A Christmas star card is sure to be received with pleasure, especially because it can be used by the recipient as a festive decoration in the future. I have saved time by using double-sided patterned paper and randomly scattered white punched snowflakes on the plain side to add the finishing touch.

christmas snowflakes
Finished size 7.5cm (3in) square

you will need...

○ Card maker's tool kit, page 8

○ Five 14cm (5½in) squares of double-sided heavyweight paper

○ Two 7.5cm (3in) squares of double-sided heavyweight paper or card for covers

○ 80cm (31½in) of 1.5cm (⅝in) wide white ribbon

○ Three plain white pony beads

○ One red star pony bead

○ Small snowflake craft punch

See also
Making card blanks, page 11

Note: The outer covers are 5mm (³⁄₈in) larger than the folded squares. As the covers need to be more robust they must be made from heavyweight paper or card.

1

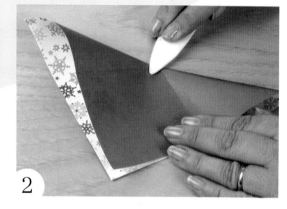

2

double-sided paper

Make your own double-sided paper by gluing two sheets of paper together before cutting to shape. For best results run one of the papers through a Xyron machine, (permanent adhesive), or use spray adhesive.

Take one of the five paper squares and, with the plain side upwards, fold it from bottom to top. Use a bone folder to crease along the fold, as shown. Open the paper back out. Now fold from left to right, use the bone folder to crease along the fold and then open back out.

Turn the paper square over so that the snowflake side is upwards and fold from corner to corner. Use the bone folder to crease along the fold. Open the paper back out.

3

4

Turn your paper square back over again so that the plain side is upwards and gently push the two sides inwards. (They will automatically fold in this way if your folds are crisp.) Repeat step 1 to 3 for each of the remaining four squares to create five folded squares in total.

Enhance the plain sides of all five folded squares by punching out small snowflakes from the white paper and securing them with a spot of glue. Fix these randomly over all the plain sides, ensuring that you do not place any over the folds.

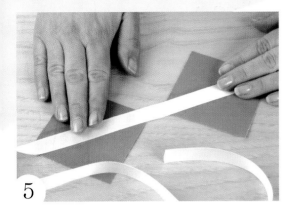

5

Lay the two small patterned squares (the covers) corner to corner with the plain side uppermost, approximately 1cm (3/8in) apart. Find the middle of the ribbon by folding it in half. Apply glue down the middle of each square, corner to corner, and with the ribbon mid point in the space between the covers, press the ribbon over the glue. Allow to dry.

6

Apply glue-stick adhesive to the top of one of your folded squares, spreading it from the middle to the outer edges. To protect the rest of the folded paper from any excess glue, slip a piece of scrap paper underneath the top layer.

<h2>stamped designs</h2>

Instead of using patterned paper, create your own patterns by using rubber stamps or drawing freehand designs on plain paper. Do this prior to folding.

7

With the point of your glued piece facing inwards towards the gap, press it centrally onto one of the outer covers to attach it. Adjust it before the glue dries, if necessary.

8

Build up a stack of folded paper squares by repeating the gluing process in the previous step. Press down firmly after attaching each folded square and check that excess glue has not resulted in any folds sticking together.

<h2>open me</h2>

To guide the recipient, write how to open the card on the outer cover or a separate piece of paper.

9

Now secure the other cover to the stack in the same way as before. You may find it easiest to hold the card while doing this.

10

Cut both ends of the ribbon to a point. Thread the ribbons through the star bead and then through a plain bead. Take one ribbon and slide on a plain bead; tie a knot in the end. Repeat for the other ribbon.

further inspiration

If you think the hanging star card can't be adapted much, you'd be wrong. Try using three folded squares of paper instead of five to create a card that will open and stand up on a flat surface. If you use four or six folded squares you'll get a different shape altogether. You can also vary the size of the star, give it decorative edges or punch out shapes to achieve a lacy effect.

See also
Strengthening papers, page 16

white wedding This elegant card is made from sheer handmade paper secured to cartridge paper for strength. It doubles as a good-luck token to give to the bride.

Make this card in the same way as the Christmas card (see page 106), but use gold peel-offs for added decoration and sew gold bead-effect cord along each fold. Finally, glue a small tassel inside that is tucked away when the card is closed and falls down when it is opened for an added surprise.

try this! Cut or punch out all the edges of the card to produce a delicate snowflake effect.

kids' korner

For a child I suggest using plain white or coloured papers for the folded squares and plain card for the two outer covers. You will need to fold the paper and then put a pencil cross onto each flat side so that your child does not decorate any areas that will be eventually glued together. Ensure that your child knows not to place any stickers over the folds and then give them the papers to decorate. Assemble your star by using paper clips to hold it together – your child can decide which is the best arrangement for the papers before securing them permanently with glue. As accuracy is essential I suggest that you assemble the card and then ask your child to complete it by decorating the outside covers.

templates

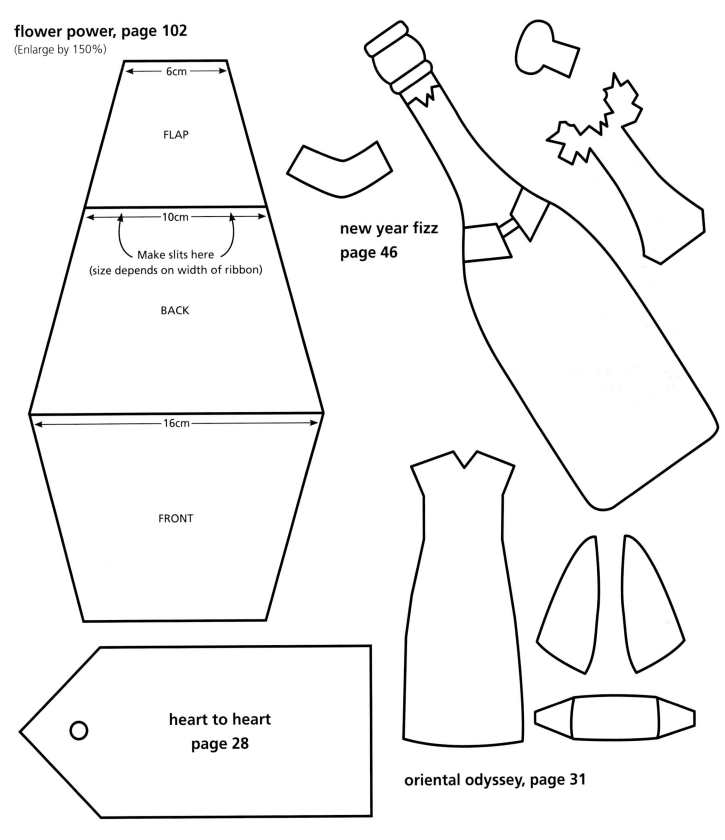

flower power, page 102
(Enlarge by 150%)

6cm

FLAP

10cm

Make slits here
(size depends on width of ribbon)

BACK

16cm

FRONT

**new year fizz
page 46**

**heart to heart
page 28**

oriental odyssey, page 31

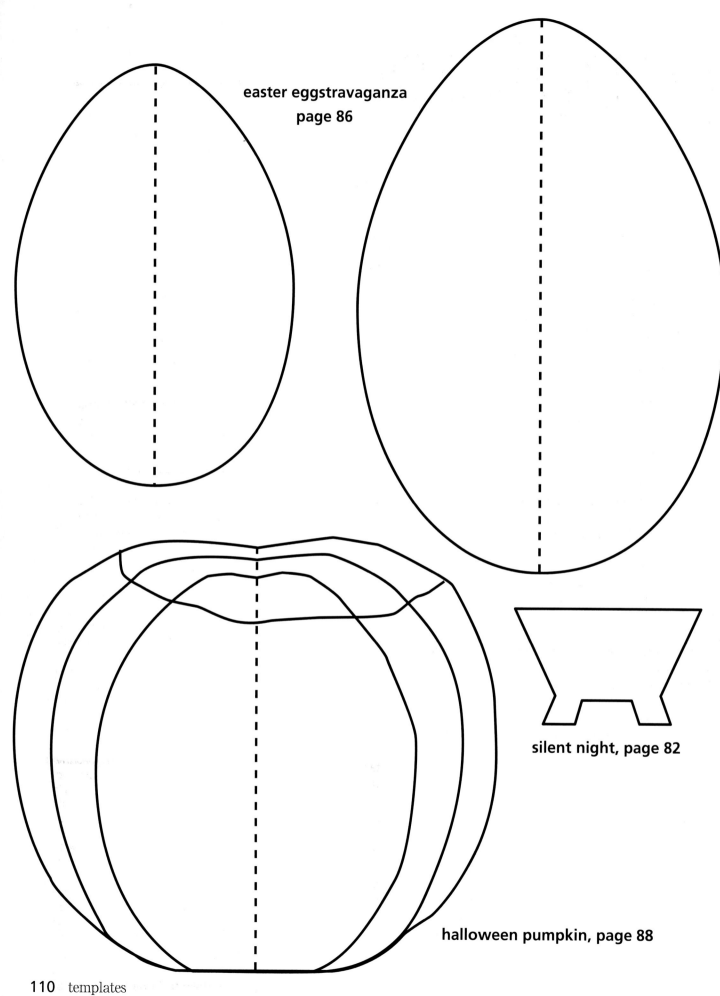

easter eggstravaganza
page 86

silent night, page 82

halloween pumpkin, page 88

suppliers

UK

F.W. Bramwell & Co. Ltd
Old Empress Mills, Empress Street, Colne
Lancs. BB8 9HU
tel:01282 860388
www.bramwellcrafts.co.uk
*UK wholesaler for most of the products
used in this book; American Crafts
(Galaxy Markers), Buttons Galore, Hero
Arts, Inkadinkado, Jones Tones, Paper
Adventures, Provo Craft, SIZZIX, Therm O
Web and Xyron.*

Courtyard Crafts
Brimstage Hall, Brimstage, Wirral CH63 6JA
tel: 0151 342 4216
e-mail: sales@courtyardcraft.co.uk
www.courtyardcraft.co.uk
Mail order service available.
*Scrapbooking papers, rubber stamping
products, peel-offs, stickers, buttons,
punches, general craft tools and materials.*

Crab Apple Crafts
Georgian House, Lady Heyes Craft Centre,
Kingsley Road, Frodsham, Cheshire
WA6 6SU
tel: 01928 787 797
e-mail: rosemary@thescrapbookstore.co.uk
www.crabapplecrafts.co.uk
Second store in Chester. Mail order service
available.
*Scrapbooking papers, rubber stamping
products, peel-offs, stickers, buttons,
punches, general craft tools and materials.*

Craft Central
Stores nationwide.
tel: 0161 980 0047
*Scrapbooking papers, rubber stamping
products, peel-offs, stickers, buttons,
punches, threads, beads, foam, general
craft tools and materials.*

Horseshoe Crafts
The Old Horseshoe, Horseshoe Lane,
Eastwick, Ellesmere, Shropshire, SY12 9JT
tel/fax: (01691) 690113
email: horseshoecrafts@hotmail.com
www.horseshoecrafts.co.uk
Mail-order service available.
*Rubber stamping products, punches,
general craft tools and materials.*

US

Michaels
Michaels Stores Inc, 8000 Bent Branch
Drive, Irving, TX 75063
tel: 972 409 1300
www.michaels.com
Large variety of art and craft materials.

A.C. Moore
130 A.C. Moore Drive
Berlin, New Jersey 08009
tel: 856 228 6700
email: micheled@acmoore.com
www.acmoore.com
Large variety of art and craft materials.

Jo-Ann
Visit the website or phone for details of
your nearest store.
tel: 1 888 739 4120
www.joann.com
Large variety of art and craft materials.

Useful Web Sites
Here is a list of suppliers and manufacturers
of craft materials suitable for card making
that you may find invaluable.
www.americancrafts.com
www.buttonsgaloreandmore.com
www.heroarts.com
www.inkadinkado.com
www.jonestones.com
www.paperadventures.com
www.provocraft.com
www.sizzix.com
www.thermoweb.com
www.xyron.com

Acknowledgments

*I am truly blessed to have the love and
unconditional support of my wonderful
family. To my husband Ian, whose
constant and continual support gave me
the ability to progress this dream. You
are there in each word and every card. To
my children Joshua and Sarah who have
encouraged me with their excitement,
suggestions and ideas. Your love of life
helped keep everything in perspective.
And to Elsie and John for all your help
and for looking after your grandchildren.
This gave me the space I needed to make
this project a success.*
I would also like to thank the following:
*• My close friends Charlotte, Dianne, Gill,
Susan and Val for being there.*
*• My hand model, Gill Williamson. Your
support was an immense help and your
company an added bonus.*
*• Alison and Tony at F.W. Bramwell & Co
Ltd for generously providing most of the
materials in this book.*
*• Karl Adamson, whose photography
brought this book alive.*
*• All at David & Charles who have made
this book a reality, especially Cheryl
Brown, Prudence Rogers, Jennifer
Proverbs and Betsy Hosegood.*

About the author

*Sue Nicholson has
always crafted
as a hobby, and
began making
and selling cards
after the birth of
her second child.
She progressed to
leading successful
workshops and
demonstrations
for a variety of
craft outlets,
including HobbyCraft. She is now a regular
contributor to Making Cards, Popular Crafts
and Practical Crafts magazines. Sue lives in
Cheshire, England, with her husband and
two children.
Sue has her own website, www.suenicholson.
com, where you can view her novelty card
gallery and pick up tips and ideas. She would
love to hear from you, so please email her:
noveltycards@suenicholson.com.*

index